THE KOLOB THEOREM

A MORMON'S VIEW OF GOD'S STARRY UNIVERSE

Lynn M. Hilton, PhD

Distributed by:

Granite Publishing and Distribution, LLC
868 North 1430 West
Orem, Utah 84057
(801) 229-9023 • Toll Free (800) 574-5779
Fax (801) 229-1924

Cover Design: Steve Gray
Page Layout and Design: Lyndell Lutes

ISBN-13: 978-1-56684-641-7
ISBN-10: 1-56684-641-2
Library of Congress Control Number:
First Printing May 2006
10 9 8 7 6 5 4 3 2 1
Printed in the United States of America

Table of Contents

CHAPTER 5: THE NUMBER OF GOD'S CREATIONS—35

CHAPTER 6: LOCATION OF THE THREE DEGREES OF GLORY—49

CHAPTER 13: DEITIES IN ADDITION TO ELOHEIM—107

SUMMARY AND CONCLUSIONS—115

BIBLIOGRAPHY—121

ABOUT THE AUTHOR—123

INDEX—125

Preface

TO THE GLORY OF GOD AND
THE FUTURE GLORY OF MANKIND

This book is written to glorify God the Father and Jesus Christ His Son, creators of our universe. We admire and stand in awe at the appearance of Their extended kingdoms. When we behold the stars we see "God moving in his majesty and power." (Doctrine and Covenants 88:47). It is also written to describe the future glory of men and women after the resurrection if they keep all the commandments of God.

FIRST COLORED PICTURE OF A GALAXY

The notion for the theory of this book came to me as a thunderbolt. It occurred to me while reading an article in *National Geographic*, entitled "First Colored Portraits of the Heavens" (William C. Miller, Research Photographer, Vol. 115, No. 5, May 1959, page 673). Here was a full-page, colored picture of our neighboring galaxy, Andromeda (see page xiii). Astronomer Miller captured this beautiful picture showing the full Andromeda galaxy, made up of three rings each of a different color. Each part was discrete and identifiable from the others by its color. There to be admired was the central nucleus of that galaxy, white, brilliant and glorious in color. A donut shaped, reddish ring made of billions of faint stars surrounded the central core. The outer ring of that galaxy, also made of countless stars, glistened with hazy blue light. Right before my eyes, in full color, was the probable design of God's universe—white, red, and blue! Celestial, Terrestrial, and Telestial!

If this were the structure of the Andromeda Galaxy, it may also be the structure of our own Milky Way Galaxy, as well as many billions of other galaxies in the extended universe. To say the least, when

I saw this picture I was more than thrilled and excited—I was in-spired! The thrill has never left me. I feel it again now as I record the memory of the experience.

WHY IS THIS BOOK IMPORTANT TO THE READER?

The Kolob Theorem allows us to see more clearly the home we lived in before we were born and the home we will live in after we die. These places appear more real; they are made of matter, some of very fine and pure matter, and exist in time and space. It helps us antici-pate the reality of the glories of our future home.

MOTHER TOLD ME ABOUT KOLOB

As a child, I overheard my mother, Ruth Naome Savage Hilton, patiently explaining about the great governing star of our universe, Kolob, to my four older brothers, as they crowded around her at the kitchen sink in our home. She quoted from the book of Abraham:

> And I saw the stars, that they were very great, and that one of them was nearest unto the throne of God; and there were many great ones which were near unto it. And the Lord said unto me: these are the governing ones; and the name of the great one is Kolob, because it is near unto me, for I am the Lord thy God; and I have set this one to govern all those which belong to the same order as that upon which thou standest. [Abraham 3:2-3]

These words entered my heart with power. I believed them to be true even as a child and I believe them to be true today. I have chosen "Kolob" as the title for this work because, from an early age, I associ-ated this word with the home of the Almighty God before whose blazing throne all things bow in humble reverence.

RESPONSIBILITY FOR THIS TEXT

If there are faults with this theory or the related ideas, I alone am to blame. The ideas of this book are for your contemplation. I do not offer them as absolute truth, but as possibilities. I will be the first to accept any new or additional light that may further establish them as true, or perhaps, require me to alter or abandon them. I do not hold myself out as a scientist, but as a man of faith: faith in God as the Father of our spirits; faith in His Son Jesus Christ as the Redeemer and Savior of the World; faith in Joseph Smith as the Prophet of the fulness of times. It was Joseph Smith who restored many of the plain and precious parts of the gospel including scriptures about the stars which we now have the joy to ponder.

EXPLANATION OF SOURCES AND REFERENCES

Footnotes and source references referred to in this book are:

- Books in the Bible are sited with the usual abbreviations.
- JST means Joseph Smith Translation of the Bible found in the footnotes and the Appendix of the Holy Bible, LDS edition.
- References to the Book of Mormon use the usual abbreviations.
- Moses means the book of Moses in the Pearl of Great Price.
- Abraham means book of Abraham in the Pearl of Great Price.
- Other sources are cited in footnotes and bibliography.

The Book of Mormon, Doctrine and Covenants, and Pearl of Great Price are the standard works of The Church of Jesus Christ of Latter-day Saints. They can be viewed or purchased at the web site: www.lds.org.

ACKNOWLEDGMENTS

I name but three of the many people who helped in the production of this book. Arlene Calkins and Nancy Mae Hilton assisted in editing. I offer many thanks to them as well as the others. Special recognition is noted here for the helpful additions made by Dr. William M.

Boushka of Texas. He was the first person to read the Kolob manuscript. His written comment was, "This is great stuff." This greatly encouraged me.

Lynn M. Hilton
May 1, 2006, Salt Lake City, Utah, USA

Five Pictures

1–M31: The Andromeda Galaxy

M31: The Andromeda Galaxy Credit & Copyright: Robert Gendler, used by permission
http://antwrp.gsfc.nasa.gov/apod/ap040718.html

Our Galaxy is thought to look much like Andromeda. The diffuse light from Andromeda is caused by the hundreds of billions of stars that compose it. The several distinct stars that surround Andromeda's image are actually stars in our Galaxy that are well in front of the background object.

This picture was fist published in *National Geographic* Magazine in full color as described in the Preface of this book. It clearly shows in colors: white from the hub (celestial kingdom), a ring of red (terrestrial kingdom) and an outer ring of blue (telestial kingdom). Andromeda is the nearest large galaxy to earth, about two million light-years away.

2–Center Regions of Our Milky Way Galaxy

Seen in natural light, the likely location of Kolob (upper center of picture) shining brightly behind a cloud (veil) of inter-stellar dust.

Center Regions of Our Milky Way Galaxy
Credit: Gemini Observatory, Peter Michaud & Kirk Pu'uohau-Pummill
http://antwrp.gsfc.nasa.gov/apod/ap030909.html

What does Kolob and the center of our Milky Way Galaxy, look like? No one knows in natural light! It is not possible to see the Galactic center in light our eyes are sensitive to because the thick dust in the plane of our Galaxy obscures it. However, if one looks in the direction of our Galaxy's center—which is toward the constellation of Sagittarius—many beautiful wonders become apparent. The center of the Milky Way is behind the center of the photo. Large dust lanes and star clouds dominate the picture.

The above picture is actually a composite of over 40 images taken by Gemini Observatory on August 19, 2003. The constellations of Scorpius and Sagittarius can be seen above the dome.

3–Center Regions of Our Milky Way Galaxy in Infrared

While obscured by interstellar dust and cannot be seen in visible light, the hub of our galaxy can be seen by infrared photography. Here is an actual picture of the center region of our Milky Way Galaxy. According to the Kolob Theorem the exact center of our galaxy is the location of Kolob and the throne of God, for "God dwells in everlasting burnings" (*Teachings of the Prophet Joseph Smith*, page 361).

Center Regions of Our Milky Way Galaxy,
Kolob in the Center,
in Infrared Light
Credit: NASA, Cosmic Background
Explorer (COBE) Project
http://antwrp.gsfc.nasa.gov/apod/ap950908.html

NASA's COBE satellite scanned the heavens at infrared wavelengths in 1990 and produced this premier view of the central region of our own Milky Way Galaxy. The Milky Way is a typical spiral galaxy with a central bulge and extended disk of stars. However, gas and dust within the disk obscure visible wavelengths of light effectively preventing clear observations of the center. Since infrared wavelengths, are less affected by the obscuring material, the Diffuse Infrared Background Experiment (DIRBE) on board COBE was able to detect infrared light from stars surrounding the galactic center and produce this image. Of course, the edge on perspective represents the view from the vicinity of our Sun, a star located in the disk about 27,000 light- years out from this center.

4−M104: The Sombrero Galaxy

From earth we can see huge pinwheel shaped galaxies which are organized external to our own Milky Way Galaxy. In fact the Hubble Telescope has observed many millions of them. Pictured here is one of the bright, nearby galaxies showing a bright center core. Could this be the location of another Kolob and the seat of another god? Notice also the dark band of interstellar dust lying in the plane of this galaxy. Could this be a veil?

M104: The Sombrero Galaxy
Located Outside Our Milky Way Showing
a Veil of Dust

Credit: T. Boroson (NOAO /USGP),
W. Keel (UA), KPNO. http://antwrp.gsfc.nasa.gov/
apod/ap951109.html

The famous Sombrero Galaxy (M104) is a spiral galaxy. The prominent dust lane and halo of stars and globular clusters give this galaxy its name. Something very energetic is going on in the Sombrero's center, as much X-ray light has been detected from it. This image was taken in blue light by the 0.9 meter telescope at Kitt Peak National Observatory.

5–Galaxies Beyond Number

Here, nearly a thousand galaxies are shown in this tiny patch of sky. The biggest 'Zoom Lens' in space allows Hubble to see deep into the universe to capture this picture. Our theory holds that each galaxy has its own god, based in its center.

Galaxies Beyond Number Exist in the Extended Universe.

Credit: NASA N. Benitez (JHU), T. Broadhurst (Racah Institute of Physics/The Hebrew University),
H. Ford (JHU), M. Clampin (STScI), G. Hartig (STScI),
G. Illingworth (UCO/Lick Observatory), the ACS Science Team and ESA.
http://hubblesite.org/gallery/album/galaxy_collection/pr2003001a/

Chapter 1

Introduction

HEAVEN IS A REAL PLACE

Heaven or the celestial kingdom is seen as a *real* place which exists in time and space. It consists of gigantic stars, (Kolob plus others) at the center, each radiating with great energy and power. The center is surrounded by millions of sanctified worlds and planets, as well as new worlds in embryo. "All spirit is matter," tangible matter, which is exceedingly "fine or pure" (D&C 131:7). While we are in mortality we cannot see spiritual matter, but if God touches our eyes we can. We reject the idea that Heaven is ethereal, cloud-like, unfathomable and unknowable; but it can be described with terms which are concrete, realistic and understandable.

THE UNIVERSE IS WELL ORGANIZED

God's Universe, although consisting of billions of suns and planets, is nevertheless orderly, fitting together in perfect unity, each part moving in harmony with each other about God's throne. There is a place in the Universe for everything, and everything is in its place.

The Prophet Joseph Smith had a clear understanding of God's Universe. He described it in astonishing detail during the A.D.1840s. We accept his ideas as coming from a divine source and are verily true. Since the time of Joseph Smith, scientists have found many similar things in the heavens.

DESCRIPTION OF THE MILKY WAY

Many discoveries of modern astronomy help us better understand the scriptures. There are many scriptures which talk about heaven, stars, suns, and planets.

In his book, *Starry Nights*, astronomer, Chet Raymo describes the Milky Way:

> When we look off into space in the direction of the flat disk of the galaxy, we see a faint wash of light from billions of stars. On a summer night, this pale band of diffuse light arches overhead from the northern to the southern horizons. It was called the Milky Way by the ancients, who had no way of knowing its true nature. (Our word "galaxy" comes from the Greek word, "gala," which means "milk.") In other myths of antiquity, it was known as a celestial river.[1]

The Kolob Theorem indicates that the spiral arm where we are located in the Milky Way Galaxy, which is seen stretched across the night sky, is indeed a celestial river made up of stars each one made by God, but only dimly seen by man. However, there are ways of learning the nature of this vast creation. We can learn by astronomy but better still is to learn from the scriptures which were dictated by the Creator Himself, who is our Heavenly Father.

EARTH IS ALIVE

Most of us think of our earth as an inert lump of rock forever circling the sun. However we assert the earth is alive. It is has a spirit, can talk and can keep God's commandments and will finally be exalted in the celestial kingdom.

PURPOSE OF THE KOLOB THEOREM

The theory of this book gives a framework upon which we can place our Latter-day Saint doctrines of heaven and eternity. Each part fits together like the interlocking pieces of a jigsaw puzzle, showing each section's proper relation to the other pieces. The entire exercise reveals an amazing pattern of gigantic size and complexity. Our universe is powerful, alive, and growing. We are forced not only to admire

---

[1] Chet Raymo, Starry Nights: *An Introduction to Astronomy for Every Night of the Year*, Prentice Hall, Englewood Cliffs, New Jersey, page 121.

the starry universe, but also to worship and praise the God of heaven who created it and who today guides it in its movement and growth.

In the least, this theory is stimulating speculation. It suggests many new approaches to old questions. In any case, several people have told me their minds have not rested since they contemplated the ideas in *The Kolob Theorem*.

CREATOR OF ALL THINGS

Both ancient and modern scriptures teach that God, working through His Son, Jesus Christ, created all things. Many examples could be given, but two will suffice:

> In the beginning was the Word, and the Word was with God, and the Word was God.
>
> The same was in the beginning with God.
>
> *All things were made by him*; and without him was not anything made that was made. [John 1:1–3, emphasis added]

> And also that you might know of the coming of Jesus Christ, the Son of God, the Father of heaven and of earth, *the Creator of all things* from the beginning. [Helaman 14:12, emphasis added]

ABRAHAM WAS AN ASTRONOMER AND TAUGHT ASTRONOMY IN EGYPT

In the Pearl of Great Price we read:

> And I, Abraham had the Urim and Thummim, which the Lord my God had given unto me, in Ur of Chaldees;
>
> And I saw the stars that they were very great, and that one of them was nearest unto the throne of God; and there were many great ones which were near unto it. [Abraham 3:1–2]

Here we read that the Urim and Thummim was used by Abraham to see through what we theorize as the veil of interstellar dust and into the very heart of the Galaxy. This is the location where the Kolob Theorem places the throne of God with Kolob in the center.

Later, Abraham had a face-to-face interview with the Lord:

Thus I, Abraham, talked with the Lord, face to face, as one man talketh with another; and he told me of the works which his hands had made;

And he said unto me: My son, my son (and his hand was stretched out), behold I will show you all these. And he put his hand upon mine eyes, and I saw those things which his hands had made, which were many; and they multiplied before mine eyes, and I could not see the end thereof.

And he said unto me: This is Shinehah, which is the sun. And he said unto me: Kokob, which is star. And he said unto me: Olea, which is the moon. And he said unto me: Kokaubeam, which signifies stars, or all the great lights, which were in the firmament of heaven.

And it was in the night time when the Lord spake these words unto me . . . .

And the Lord said unto me: Abraham, I show these things unto thee before ye *go into Egypt, that ye may declare all these words."* [Abraham 3:11–15, emphasis added]

Thus, the Lord showed Abraham "those things his hands had made," that Abraham might teach them in Egypt. According to the Kolob Theorem, Abraham was shown the Great Milky Way Galaxy; he drew it as a circle and was commanded to tell others about it. Notice the striking centralized position of Kolob in Facsimile No. 2:1 in the book of Abraham. Illustrating that God dwells in the "midst of all things?" (D&C 88:13). Is Facsimile No. 2 a star chart of our galaxy? Notice that the explanation of Facsimile 2:5 tells us that numbers 22 and 23 represent two of the great stars near Kolob. See how close these are to Kolob in this round picture.

Indeed, what did Abraham teach the Egyptians about astronomy? Surely, not about black holes or quasars. But he did go to the trouble of drawing Facsimile No. 3, which shows him "reasoning on principles of astronomy . . . in the court of Pharaoh." Reasoning connotes more than just explaining. Why was he reasoning with them?

Perhaps to present the gospel.

The Kolob Theorem is presented for your contemplation. These ideas are only theories. They are the result of the author's attempts to study the scriptures and astronomy, as suggested by the Lord, and to try to understand them at least in part. We pretend no revelation, but do await the glorious day, spoken of by the Lord to Joseph Smith:

> A time to come in the which nothing shall be withheld, whether there be one God, or many gods, they shall be manifest.
>
> All thrones and dominions, principalities and powers, shall be revealed and set forth upon all who have endured valiantly for the gospel of Jesus Christ. [D&C 121:28–29]

OUR HEAVENLY FATHER HAS A FATHER

It is equally clear from the teachings of latter-day prophets, that Eloheim, our Father, was once a mortal being working out His salvation upon another earth in subjection to His Father. Joseph Smith taught: "It is the first principle of the gospel to know for a certainty the Character of God, and to know that . . . he was once a man like us; yea, that God himself, the father of us all, dwelt on an earth."[2]

President Joseph Fielding Smith said, "Our Father in Heaven, according to the Prophet, had a Father, and since there has been a condition of this kind through all eternity, each Father had a Father."[3] Brigham Young explained that "there never was a time when there were not Gods and worlds and when men were not passing through the same ordeals that we are now passing through."[4]

Surely, these divine progenitors of Eloheim are deities in their own right, with worlds, powers, kingdoms, and creations of their own. None of which could have been created by Eloheim or Jehovah.

---

[2] *Teachings of the Prophet Joseph Smith,* pp 345-46.
[3] Joseph Fielding Smith, *Doctrines of Salvation,* Bookcraft, 1955, Vol 2, page 47.
[4] *Deseret News,* 16 Nov. 1859, page 290.

When the Almighty says all things were created by Jesus Christ, it is our opinion that He is limiting this statement to His creations, since the council in heaven, where the Plan of God was first formally presented to His spirit children, and Christ was assigned to be the Creator, as well as the Savior. Thus started the process of creation of the Father's plan for His own galaxy or universe.

This brings many questions to mind. What is the domain of Eloheim, our Father? How far do His creations extend? Where is Kolob, our Father's dwelling place? Where are the creations, dominions, and thrones of the other deities? This is a tall order. It may sound preposterous at the outset. In answer to these queries, we propose the Kolob Theorem.

This Theorem outlines the overall structure of Heavenly Father's creations, with the purpose, nature, and location of each part. It identifies the Milky Way Galaxy as the only creation of our Father. It provides insight into the structure of the hub of our galaxy. The theory identifies the location of the throne of God and the three degrees of glory; it explains where the earth was formed and where it is headed. It provides a mechanism for the establishment of the seats of future deities, as the children of Eloheim enter into their exaltation such as Abraham, Isaac and Jacob (D&C 132:37) plus a host to follow. It also explains the possible location of Eloheim's fathers', brothers', uncles', and cousins' kingdoms, which must exist somewhere.

The basic idea of the Kolob Theorem places the celestial kingdom in the hub of the Milky Way Galaxy; that an intermediate, doughnut-shaped ring surrounding this hub is the location of the terrestrial kingdom; and an outer ring surrounding the terrestrial zone is the location of the telestial kingdom. Our sun and its planets now occupy a position in this third, outer or telestial zone. The earth was created in the celestial kingdom, in the core of the galaxy, and migrated through the terrestrial zone (the Garden of Eden period) perhaps to take up its present position about the sun in the telestial kingdom. Conversely, when earth time is counted no longer, the earth will depart from its orbit about the sun and return through the terrestrial zone (the millennial period) then to resume its original place in the celestial kingdom.

AN APOSTLE URGES US TO STUDY SCRIPTURES DESCRIBING THE HEAVENS

Brother Orson Pratt spoke of kingdoms upon kingdoms throughout the immensity of space and then said:

> Perhaps you may ask me why I dwell on this . . . subject. In answer, why did the Lord dwell upon it forty-two years ago, if he did not want us, in some measure, to understand it? Would he speak at random? Would he give a revelation without expecting that the people would even try to understand it? If the Lord wished us to understand something, and condescended to reveal something, why should we . . . think that we are stepping over our bounds in trying to comprehend approximately what the Lord desired us to understand . . . It is an old sectarian whim and notion, to suppose that we must not try to understand revelation.
>
> . . . Do not suppose, however, that those first principles [of the gospel] are the only ones to be learned; do not become stereotyped in your feelings, and think that you must always dwell upon them and proceed no further. If there be knowledge concerning the future, . . . the present, . . . [the] past, or any species of knowledge that would be beneficial to the mind of man, let us seek it; and that which we cannot obtain by using the light which God has placed within us, by using our reasoning powers, by reading books, or by human wisdom alone, let us seek to a higher source—to that Being who is filled with knowledge, and who has given laws to all things and who, in his wisdom, goodness, justice and mercy, controls all things according to their capacity, and according to the various spheres and conditions in which they are placed.[5]

---

[5] Orson Pratt, March 14, 1875, Salt Lake City, 16th Ward, reported by David W. Evans

Elder Pratt encourages the Saints to study the subjects hinted at in the revelations of God. Many principles and truths have been revealed by the Lord concerning astronomy. In the Doctrine and Covenants 88:79, the Lord expressly commands the Saints to study the heavens. Surely there must be something we are supposed to discover, or why else this commandment?

Chapter 2

The Kolob Theorem
and Twelve Corollaries

STATEMENT OF THE KOLOB THEOREM

All the creations of our God, Heavenly Father, are located in the sublime and orderly limits of the Milky Way Galaxy. God sits enthroned in the center of the galaxy, in the "midst of all things," (D&C 88:13) and controls all the kingdoms His hands have made.

COROLLARIES TO THE KOLOB THEOREM

The following extrapolations of the basic theory are offered as possible explanations:

COROLLARY 1: Location of the Celestial Kingdom

In addition to God's throne, the celestial worlds of Heavenly Father, and indeed the total celestial kingdom, are in the glorious hub, or central region of the Milky Way Galaxy.

COROLLARY 2: Emissions From the Hub of Our Galaxy Obscured by a Veil

The radiations of God's light, which proceed forth from His presence to fill the immensity of space (D&C 88:12) are filtered through veils of interstellar dust, which block our mortal view of the celestial kingdom. Whenever you penetrate this "veil," you are within the fiery environment of the celestial kingdom.

COROLLARY 3: The Number of God's Creations

While the number of God's creations is beyond the ability of man to count, each one is known unto God. These creations are of finite number at any instant in time and consist of about 150 billion stars, plus their associated planets as presently exist in the Milky Way Galaxy.

COROLLARY 4: Location of the Three Degrees of Glory

The terrestrial and telestial kingdoms are located in successive concentric, doughnut-shaped rings, round about the celestial kingdom or central hub of the galaxy; that our sun and earth are now located in the outer or telestial ring of the Milky Way galaxy.

COROLLARY 5: Location of Outer Darkness

"Outer Darkness," the place of Satan's final banishment (D&C 76:44–49) with the sons of perdition, is beyond the reaches of the Milky Way Galaxy, where there is no light or heat, no suns or stars.

COROLLARY 6: Sequence of Earth's Development

Our planet earth was first formed in an orbit of Kolob in the celestial core of the galaxy. It migrated out through the terrestrial ring (the Garden of Eden period), and took up its present position, in an orbit of the sun, for its mortal, telestial probation. The earth will return by being pulled away from the sun, passing again through the terrestrial ring (the millennial period), and finally regaining its original orbit about Kolob in the celestial kingdom.

COROLLARY 7: Other Mortal Worlds Within the Milky Way

Heavenly Father has many other worlds which follow the same pattern as earth and now exist in one of several stages of this progression; that many are now in their mortal period and are peopled with beings who look, act, and associate together as we do, for they also, as we, are children of Heavenly Father

COROLLARY 8: Speed of Transportation

There must exist a speed of transportation of heavenly beings, faster than the speed of light, a speed such as the speed of thought.

COROLLARY 9: Counting Time

Heavenly Father has a system of time—a clock, shall we say, similar to ours but ticking more slowly; in ratio as one is to 365,000. Earth time is experienced only during the telestial probation of the earth. In addition, a terrestrial "clock" must exist to measure the Garden of Eden and the Millennium periods.

COROLLARY 10: In Heaven's Image

Things on this earth are patterned after, or even descended from, heavenly originals, and we can understand heaven in part by studying this earth. God himself lives in a real place composed of actual materials on a crystal sphere—a great Urim and Thummim.

COROLLARY 11: Children of Heavenly Father Become Deities

Faithful children of Heavenly Father who follow His celestial laws will have the opportunity, after their resurrection and exaltation in the celestial kingdom, to form new galaxies and Kolobs—each with a new hub with suns and worlds as places of residence for their own countless spirit offspring giving rise to a new generation of gods.

COROLLARY 12: Deities in addition to Eloheim

The unnumbered billions of external galaxies beyond our Milky Way are not the creations of Eloheim, but each has its own deity, its own celestial kingdom in its fiery core, with terrestrial and telestial kingdoms round about. Perhaps galaxies, in turn, cluster and revolve about ever higher centers.

Chapter 3

Location of the Celestial Kingdom

COROLLARY 1:

LOCATION OF THE CELESTIAL KINGDOM

In addition to God's Throne, the celestial worlds of Heavenly Father, and indeed the total celestial kingdom, are in the glorious hub, or central region of our Milky Way Galaxy.

GOSPEL PRINCIPLES, THE BASIS OF THIS CHAPTER

Abraham saw, by the Urim and Thummim, the huge star Kolob, that it was "nearest unto the throne of God" (Abraham 3:2); that Kolob was the first of all of God's creations (Abraham Facsimile 2:1); that "Kolob is the greatest" of all the stars (Abraham 3:16), and that it "govern[s] all" the stars "which belong to the same order as that upon which thou [Abraham] standest [earth]" (Abraham 3:3). The scriptures also establish that God's throne is in the "midst of all things" (D&C 88:13). Likely this means at the center of the Milky Way Galaxy.

GOD IS AT THE CENTER

God's throne, His headquarters or governing place, is not off to one side, but where one would logically expect Him to be; right in the middle of His creations. Consider the following quotations:

... God who sitteth upon his throne, who is in the bosom of *eternity, who is in the midst of all things.* [D&C 88:13, emphasis added]

"He comprehendeth all things, and all things are before him, and all things are round about him .... [D&C 88:41, emphasis added]

To find our heavenly home, we must look for a "center" place. It will be a place "nigh unto Kolob" and the other great governing stars, which control or govern the earth, for Abraham said:

I saw the stars, that they were very great, and that one of them was nearest unto the throne of God; and there were many great ones which were near unto it;

And the Lord said unto me: These are the governing ones; and the name of the great one is Kolob, because it is near unto me, for I am the Lord thy God: I have set this one to govern all those which belong to the same order as that upon which thou standest. [Abraham 3:2–3]

KOLOB IS THE GREATEST STAR

Our sun governs the earth, but is by no means "the mighty one" among the stars. Our sun, in turn, is governed by and is proceeding in a grand orbit about the core of the Milky Way Galaxy. Here we have a gigantic aggregation of stars of such immense size and complexity as to be truly beyond our comprehension. Here in the center is a concentration of ancient, huge stars of such amazing mass and radiations as to identify it as the most exotic spot in our universe. The theory of this book identifies the core of the galaxy as the "circling flames of fire; also the blazing throne of God" (D&C 137:2–3). Kolob, Heavenly Father's first and mightiest star, is at the center, and the "globe" (D&C 130:7) or Urim and Thummim upon which He resides (see D&C 130:8) is near unto it, perhaps in orbit about it.

Some findings of modern astronomy which tend to support the Kolob Theorem:

CLUSTERS OF STARS AT THE GALACTIC
CORE OF THE MILKY WAY

The core of the Galaxy, which is largely veiled from our view by clouds of dust, is located in the direction of the Constellation Sagittarius. In the northern hemisphere it is low on the southern horizon on a summer's night. According to Dr. Harlow Shapley of Harvard University, many of the stars in the Galaxy's central region are in tight rotation around the center, as shown by their blinking light. He says,

> Hundreds of variable stars and many clusters and diffuse nebula have been studied in the Sagittarius area. Much remains to be done on the stars of the central mass (or galactic nucleus) that appears to be located 30,000 light-years distant. It controls the motion of our sun and neighboring stars and thus determines the length of the cosmic [galactic] year.[6]

CENTRAL STARS ARE UNIQUE

In discussing the stars in the central region of the galaxy, Bok and Bok conclude: "The stars that populate the nucleus are very different (population II type of stars) from those that are found in the outer spiral regions (population I type stars)."[7]

British astronomer Fred Hoyle reports:

> The stars in the elliptical galaxies and the stars in the nuclei of the spirals are old stars like the stars in the globular clusters. In contrast, the highly luminous blue giants and super giants are young stars. Young stars are found only in the arms of the spirals.[8]

Our theory would require such a distinction, for the stars in the nucleus must be of a celestial type created first and those of the outer regions of a terrestrial or telestial type and created later.

---

[6] Harlow Shapley, *The Galaxies,* Harvard University Press, Cambridge, MA, 1961, page 96.
[7] Bok and Bok, *The Milky Way* 5th Edition, Harvard University Press, Cambridge, MA, 1981, page 84-86.
[8] Fred Hoyle, *Frontiers of Astronomy,* New York, Harpers, 1955.

THE NUCLEI OF EXTERNAL GALAXIES

While a direct view of our own nuclei is mostly obscured by dust, it is possible to see many exact details of a celestial core by observing the hub of our sister galaxy, Andromeda—M31 (see page xiii). Astronomer Joseph Ashbrook reported on photographs of this part of the sky taken with a 30-inch refractor telescope. He explained that usual pictures of Andromeda overexpose the central core in order to display the galaxy's spiral arms. This technique has hidden a dense, star-cluster core in the exact center, 4.5 seconds of arc in diameter. *"This feature should be carefully distinguished from the central condensation or general brightening of Andromeda . . . towards the midpoint."*[9]

If all galaxies are similarly formed, the core of the Milky Way Galaxy would also possess a tightly packed system of ancient, huge stars in the very heart of the galaxy. Of this, we have an independent corroboration.

MASS OF OUR GALAXY'S CORE
AND BLACK HOLES

Bok and Bok, previously cited, conclude, "There may well be a central core of high density inside the large nuclear spheroid, and the total mass of this core may be as high as one-tenth of that of the whole galaxy."[10] Clearly the mass of one Kolob star, great as it may be, would not be sufficient to control our galactic system. It requires a dense concentration of "great ones," as seen in Andromeda to accumulate such a controlling mass and as set forth in Abraham 3:2.

Astronomers have recently found evidence of super massive activities at the center of several external galaxies. These are called black holes. A black hole is defined as a compact energy source of enormous strength of the order of a billion solar masses; that is a billion times

---

[9] Joseph Ashbrook, *The Nucleus of the Andromeda Nebula,* Sky and Telescope, February 1968, page 97.

[10] Bok and Bok, ibid, page 232.

larger than our sun. One of them, found in the center of the giant elliptical galaxy M 87, is believed to be as large as three billion solar masses. These are identified as black holes.

It is possible to discern that the centers of these large objects are rotating at high speed. One measurement of the radial velocities near the nucleus of Galaxy M 84, in the area of Virgo, shows a speed of rotation of 400 kilometers per second at a distance of only 25 light-years from the center.

These huge objects are thought to draw into them many near by stars using their enormous gravity. Some material is ejected in long jets of particles of matter which rise perpendicular to the plane of the hole. One jet of this exotic material has been measured spewing this material in a straight jet, to a distance of 6,500 light-years from the nucleus of Galaxy 87. This distance is approximately the same as one fourth the distance from earth to the center of the Milky Way.

Scientists have determined the mass of some galaxies is far greater than the sum of all the radiant stars in them. They refer to the extra mass as "dark matter," but no one is sure what dark matter really is. We wonder if spirit and intelligence could account for this extra mass? We know that all spirit is fine or pure matter (D&C 131:7).

This information and a fuller discussion on Black Holes can be found at web site: http://csep10.phys.utk.edu/astr162/lect/active/smblack.html

This new information leads us to ask ourselves:

- Could a black hole exist in the heart of every galaxy?
- Could there be a black hole at the center of the Milky Way?
- Could this be a recycling of old worlds into new ones, as referred "as one world passes away . . . so shall another come" (Moses 1:38).
- Could a black hole also be called "Kolob"?
- Could this answer the puzzle of how worlds, moons and suns get their initial rotation and speed to revolve?

- Could this be the way Kolob sends "power" and "light" to the galaxy as referred to in Abraham Facsimile 2:5?
- Could this process be one of the ways Kolob provides the material used in the creation of this earth?

THE SIZE OF KOLOB

To obtain some idea of the size of Kolob, which is described as "the great one" (Abraham 3:3), consider the double star Epsilon Aurigae. One of its stars is a yellow super giant 250 times larger than our sun. "But its companion is even bigger—3000 times the size of the sun."[11] Since Kolob is "the great one," it must be even larger than Epsilon Aurigae.

FIFTEEN FIXED STARS IN THE CORE

The Prophet spent much time studying the astronomy revealed in the book of Abraham. He patiently recorded what appears to be the meaning of certain hieroglyphics. Under the heading of the Fifth Degree of Jeh-oh-eh, Joseph spoke of three governing stars, which work in conjunction with twelve others to form the governing power. This hierarchy is strikingly reminiscent of the First Presidency and the Quorum of the Twelve. (But then, are not all things in heaven and earth supposed to bear witness of God?). Under this degree the Prophet wrote:

> The earth under the governing power of Oleblish, Enish-go-on-dosh, and Kae-e-vanrash, which are the grand key, or in other words, the governing power, which governs the fifteen fixed stars . . . that govern the earth, sun, and moon (which have their power in one) with the other twelve moving planets of this system. Oleblish, Enish-go-on-dosh and Kae-e-vanrash are the three grand central powers that govern all the other creations, which have been sought out by the most aged of all the fathers, since the beginning of creation.[12]

---

[11] Roy A. Gallant, *Exploring the Universe,* Garden City, New York: Garden City Books, 1956.
[12] Joseph Smith, *Egyptian Alphabet and Grammar,* Utah Lighthouse Book Store, 135 SW Temple, Salt Lake City, Utah, 1966, page 24.

The fifteen fixed planets or stars, which are mentioned in our Pearl of Great Price (Abraham Facsimile 2:5), are then named by the Prophet, including Kolob and the three named above:

1. Kolob	6. Zip	11. Oansli
2. Oleblish	7. Vusel	12. Kible
3. Enish-go-on-dosh	8. Vauiste	13. Shineflis
4. Kae-e-vanrash	9. Waine	14. Flis
5. Lindi	10. Way-ho-ox-oan	15. Os

What astonishing information about the place near unto God's throne and likely the center of the Milky Way!

Joseph continues under the heading of the second part of the fourth degree of Veh-kli-flos-isis. "It signifies less power in its affinity with the first, second, third, and fourth fixed stars, not having power to govern another but having power in affinity with another to govern."[13] This passage appears to indicate that to achieve a mass sufficient to hold the galaxy together by gravity it is necessary to collect in close proximity to each other many of the great stars—that is, "to have their power in one or in affinity." As Abraham said, "These are the governing ones; and the name of the great one is Kolob . . . and there are many great ones near to it" (Abraham 3:2).

FIXED STARS

The idea of a fixed or stationary star is hard to conceive, unless such stars form the exact center of the galaxy with all other stars moving about that "fixed" point. Further evidence that these stars are at the galaxy's nucleus are in the Prophet's explanation, "the central powers that govern all the other creations of Eloheim."[14] He also wrote, "let this be the center for light . . . and the light of the fifteen fixed stars center there."[15]

---

[13] Ibid., page 28
[14] Ibid., page 24
[15] Ibid., page 25

PROS AND CONS

Not all Latter-day Saints accept the center of the Milky Way as the place of Kolob.[16] These authors identify Kolob as located in a higher center around which the hub of the Milky Way Galaxy revolves, called the metagalactic center.

On the other hand, J. Reuben Clark, Jr., held the hub of our galaxy as the site of Kolob. He said:

> Our own galaxy has its own; indeed is its own heaven . . . In reference to this hub group of stars around which the other units of the galaxy revolve, we might well recall what God said to Abraham "These are the governing ones; and the name of the great one is Kolob . . . I have set this one to govern all those which belong to the same order as that upon which thou standest" (Abraham 3:3).[17]

Also, Elders George Reynolds and Janne M. Sjodahl offered the core of the Milky Way as the place of Kolob, for "as the moon revolves round the earth and the earth and other planets of this solar system revolve about the sun, so has the sun a center about which it revolves, *Kolob*."[18]

CONCLUSION

Our discussion leads us to conclude God's throne lies in the center of the Milky Way Galaxy about 27,000 light-years from us on earth. We have seen this very spot in the heavens has enough mass to hold, by gravity, all the revolving suns with their solar systems of planets in orbit. Recent astrological finds confirm what we have heard for years about the structure of the heavens from our prophets. This simple fact greatly increases our faith.

---

[16] M. Garfield Cook, *Everlasting Burnings,* Phoenix Publishing Inc., Salt Lake City, Utah, 1981, Footnote 107.
[17] BYU Selected Speeches, 1951, J. Reuban Clark, Jr. *What Was This Jesus,* published by BYU Extension Publications.
[18] George Reynolds and Janne M. Sjodahl, *Commentary on the Pearl of Great Price,* 1965, page 309, emphasis added.

The Kolob Theorem first calls for fifteen fixed stars at the core of the galaxy. It then requires hundreds of additional "great ones" (stars) to be clustered about these central, fixed stars, followed by a mantle of thousands and then millions of stars all in orbit about the galaxy's core. These may all be the celestial worlds of Heavenly Father. Many of these worlds may have completed their mortal probation and now are quickened and celestialized as they return home to resume their native orbit about Kolob. Others may be newly created, spiritual worlds in preparation for a corporal existence. All these constitute the celestial kingdom in the burning central regions of the Milky Way.

Chapter 4

Emissions from the Hub of Our Galaxy Obscured by a Veil

COROLLARY 2:
EMISSIONS FROM THE HUB OF THE GALAXY OBSCURED BY A VEIL

The radiations of God's light, which proceed forth from His presence (D&C 88:12) are filtered through veils of interstellar dust, which block our mortal view of the celestial kingdom. Whenever you penetrate this "veil," you are within the fiery environment of the celestial kingdom.

GOSPEL PRINCIPLES, THE BASIS OF THIS CHAPTER

Natural man would wither and die in the presence of God, but if he looked with "spiritual eyes," as Moses did when God's glory came upon him, he could "behold his face, for [he] was transfigured before him" (Moses 1:11). The glory, bright light and enormous radiations do proceed forth from God "to fill the immensity of space" (D&C 88:12). Mortal Earth is hidden and largely protected from this burning glory by a veil.

VEIL OF THE TEMPLE

There are two aspects to this part of the theory, relative to the veil between the earth and the celestial center. The first is to keep the intense radiations of God's glory from burning mankind and the earth. The second is to keep fallen man, now in a telestial order, from looking into heaven and being in the presence of God while still in his probationary state.

We read of a "veil" in Herod's temple in Jerusalem that was "rent in twain" upon the crucifixion of the Savior (Matthew 27:51). The veil, or curtain, of that ancient temple (and of the preceding Solomon's temple and Moses' tabernacle) symbolized this barrier between God and man. It was intended to keep the priest of Aaron outside of the Holy of Holies until the appointed time when he alone parted the veil and entered into that holy place. (Notice in these Aaronic Priesthood Temples only the priest passes through the veil, not the congregation.)

The Lord Jesus said to the elders of the Church:

> And again, verily I say unto you that it is your privilege, and a promise I give unto you that have been ordained unto this ministry, that inasmuch as you strip yourselves from jealousies and fears, and humble yourselves before me, for ye are not sufficiently humble, the veil shall be rent and you shall see me and know that I am. [D&C 67:10]

It is a widely held belief among some great religions of the earth that when a man passes through a veil he enters into the presence of God.

A VEIL SHIELDS THE EARTH

Again, from the Doctrine and Covenants, the Lord promised that the veil "which hideth the earth shall be taken off, and all flesh shall see me together.

"And every corruptible thing . . . shall be consumed;

"And . . . shall melt in the fervent heat; and all things shall become new" (D&C 101:23–25). This passage clearly shows the shielding effect of the veil.

Considerable and astonishing detail about this barrier between the earth and heaven is offered in the Prophet Joseph's *Egyptian*

Alphabet and Grammar. His comments recorded under the heading, Fifth Degree of Flosisis reads:

> God has said, Let this be the center for light, and *let there be bounds that it may not pass.* He hath set a cloud round about in the heavens, and the light of the grand governing . . . fifteen fixed stars center there . . . *So God has set the bounds of light lest it pass over and consume the planets.*[19]

Consider that nearly 150 years ago, long before science had any idea of the structure of the Universe, God's prophet said that there exists "clouds round about in the heavens" for "bounds of light" from the concentrated emissions "of the fifteen fixed stars" in the center place, and that the purpose of these clouds is to keep the planets from being consumed. What profound insight! We stand with awe and respect for Joseph's prophetic powers.

VEILS OF DUST INSIDE THE GALAXY

Only in our generation has mankind stumbled on to this idea earlier stated by Joseph in his *Egyptian Alphabet and Grammar.* E.E. Barnard and Max F.J.C. Wolf, in our day, after studying the dark patches in the Milky Way for many years, finally concluded that these "empty" spaces in the heavens were not holes.

They did not indicate the absence of matter, but rather the presence of matter, vast clouds of dust particles that absorbed and blocked off the light of the stars that lay behind them, much as the clouds in the earth's atmosphere absorbed and blocked off the light of the sun behind them.[20]

This interstellar dust is thought to be very fine in diameter—only a few thousandths or hundredths of an inch. Bernhard, et al., said, "Inasmuch as the edges of the [dust] masses are often sharp, as in the

---

[19] Joseph Smith, *Egyptian Alphabet and Grammar,* ibid page 25, emphasis added.
[20] Isaac Asimov, *The Universe: From Flat Earth to Quasar,* Walker and Company, NY, 1966, page 73.

horse-head nebula, it is concluded that likely the clouds of this material are held together by gravitation."[21]

For evidence of these dark patches of dust that mask the stars behind them, see the accompanying picture on page xiv, which is a view of the Milky Way Galaxy in the general direction of the hub. The black patches, oddly shaped, are part of the dust in the region of Sagittarius, blocking our view.

These vast clouds of dust are discussed by Professor Shapley of Harvard:

> Much of the obscuring material that conceals the galactic nucleus is at no great distance, only a few hundred or a thousand light-years away, and it probably has nothing to do with the nucleus itself. It is in part the dust that lies between the spiral arms. But wherever the obscuring material may be located, it effectively conceals some of the nucleus, and probably dims it all to a measurable degree. Beyond the center, there must be much dust, for in its general direction, no external galaxies show through . . . . We suspect sometimes that there may be around our galaxy a continuous peripheral ring of obscuration.[22]

It appears, therefore, that what the Prophet Joseph Smith described has actually been discovered as this band of obscuring matter stretching through the galaxy. Its proximity to earth suggests it likely is the curtain separating the telestial zone of the galaxy from the terrestrial. There is good reason to believe there exists another veil between the terrestrial and the celestial zones (see diagram, page 50).

VEILS OF DUST INSIDE EXTERNAL GALAXIES

The shape and size of rings of obscuring matter is quite evident in several galaxies outside the Milky Way. They are so distant that

[21] Bernhard, Bennett, Rice, *New Handbook of the Heavens* Hubert J. Bernhard, Dorothy A. Bennett and Hugh S. Rice: Moon Stars Astronomy, Whittlesey House, McGraw-Hill Company, New York, 1964, page 143.

[22] Harlow Shapley, *Galaxies,* Harvard University Press, 1961, pages 91, 96.

they can be seen in single view. Those tilted to be seen in cross section best show their veils. For example, the *Hubble Atlas of Galaxies* contains two photographs of Messier 64 Galaxy in Comma Berenices showing clearly the dust. Allan Sandoge calls it Sb because of the great *lane of dust near its center.* M64 is often called the "black-eyed galaxy," because of this dark feature. According to our theory, this veil of dust lying near a galaxy's lustrous center, separates the terrestrial and celestial zones.

The Galaxy known as Messier 81 in Ursa Major, when photographed by the 200-inch Mt. Palomar telescope shows two veils on the side of the galaxy nearest the viewer. Perhaps the inner veil separates the celestial from the terrestrial, and the next veil parts the terrestrial from the telestial.

The picture on page xiii of the Spiral Nebula in Andromeda seen partly on edge is taken by the 60-inch Mount Wilson Observatory telescope. A wide-range band of light-obstructing matter stretches across our view of the galaxy. Notice especially how the fires of the celestial core are effectively shielded.

One of the most beautiful sights in all the heavens is the Sombrero Galaxy, Messier 104 (see page xvi). Observe the sharply defined ring of obscuring matter about the plane of this galaxy.

Can anyone see such evidence and doubt the inspiration of Joseph Smith's statement that there exists "clouds round about" as "bounds of light lest it pass over and consume the planets"?

NO DUST IN THE HUB

Fred Hoyle points out, "When we turn to galaxies that contain dust clouds, we find a curious situation. Dust scarcely ever is found in the center regions, but only in the flattened outer part."[23] This may be strange to Mr. Hoyle, but it is not at all strange to those willing to consider the Kolob Theorem.

---

[23] Fred Hoyle, *Frontiers of Astronomy,* New York, Harper's, 1955, page 215.

THE LIGHT THAT FILLS
THE IMMENSITY OF SPACE

The Lord revealed to Joseph Smith that the light of Christ is:

The light which shineth, which giveth you light, is through him who enlighteneth your eyes, which is the same light that quickeneth your understandings,

Which light proceedeth forth from the presence of God to fill the immensity of space—

The light which is in all things, which giveth life to all things, which is the law by which all things are governed, even the power of God who sitteth upon his throne, who is in the bosom of eternity, who is in the midst of all things. [D&C 88:11–13]

Apparently, these radiations include all spectral bands known to modern science, plus some marvelous radiations not yet completely understood (i.e., radiations which "quicken your understandings" and which give "life to all things").

TO BORROW OR RECEIVE POWER FROM KOLOB

In the great revelation on astronomy given to Abraham and again to Joseph Smith, we are informed that light radiates out from Kolob to give power to the sun, moon, and earth through the medium of Kae-e-vanrash and Kli-flos-is-es, two of the 15 fixed stars (see Abraham Facsimile 2:5). Joseph Smith, in his *Egyptian Alphabet and Grammar*, informs us that "the light of the 15 fixed stars centers there and from there [the light] is drawn by the heavenly bodies according to their proportions."[24]

Astronomers have yet to confirm that our sun, for example, is renewed or refueled by such outpourings from the heavenly center. However, Isaac Asimov stated "the amount of energy represented by this [solar] radiation is simply colossal, and virtually all of it pours outward in all directions, at an enormous rate, into the vast spaces

---

[24] Joseph Smith, *Egyptian Alphabet and Grammar*, ibid, page 25.

beyond the solar system [but within the galaxy]. Moreover, as nearly as we can tell, virtually none of it ever returns."[25] Latter-day Saints suspect that the sun (indeed, all the suns) is generously replenished by radiations from Kolob through the medium of Kae-e-vanrash, and in due time, we may come to understand this process.

THE RADIATION SPECTRUM

Visible light is but a narrow part of the electromagnetic spectrum known to modern science. There are instruments used to detect unseen radiations such as gamma rays, x-rays, infrared rays, microwaves, and radio waves, which are all beyond the limits of the human eye. Astronomy advanced greatly when sophisticated instruments scanned the heavens looking for these forms of energy which before were invisible.

THE STRONGEST RADIO SOURCE

The science of radio astronomy was founded in 1932 by the "discovery of extra terrestrial radio noise at a wavelength of 14.7 meters, which came in strongest from the direction of the center of our Milky Way system."[26] While there are other beacons of radio radiations, such as our sun, and other discrete sources both within and without our galaxy, the most powerful and sustained radiation in the sky, emanates from the core of our galaxy which we call Kolob.

THE STRONGEST INFRARED SOURCE

See infrared picture of the hub of our Galaxy on page xv.

Until a few years ago, little was known of heavenly radiations in the infrared. Astronomers G. Neugebauer and Eric Becklin report new discoveries of infrared radiations from cooler objects in the sky. They say, "Celestial objects whose temperatures might range from 2000 degrees Kelvin, down to room temperature or even lower" can

---

[25] Isaac Asimov, ibid, page 103.
[26] Bok & Bok, ibid, page 195.

now be studied by high altitude balloons or earth-orbiting satellites. "The reason is that objects in this temperature range emit the bulk of their energy at wavelengths between one micron and 1000 microns (one millimeter), which lie in the infrared part of the electromagnetic spectrum and are therefore largely blocked by the earth's atmosphere." They summarize years of study with the assertion:

> The nucleus of our galaxy, which is invisible even with the largest optical telescopes, is actually a conglomeration of millions of stars. It stands out so conspicuously at wavelengths of 20 and 100 microns, however, that it seems likely that sources more exotic than ordinary stars are contributing to the infrared emission.[27]

We suspect that there are unusual stars in the center with profound radiations emanating from them, Eloheim's bright throne, in a band of the spectrum not visible to the eye and not yet well understood by man.

They continue their analysis of this unique spot in the sky:

> In the infrared, the galactic center stands out strongly. At two microns, it is likely that we are observing the infrared flux from millions of stars concentrated in the galactic nucleus. The strong radiation observed at 20 microns is too powerful, however, to represent the added output of even millions of stars. The 20-micron radiation from the galactic nucleus is concentrated in the core six or seven light-years in diameter, corresponding roughly to .02 percent of the distance from us to the nucleus of the galaxy. The energy distribution of this core rises steeply between 5 and 20 microns and probably peaks at a wavelength beyond 50 microns. High-resolution infrared maps made by us with the 200-inch Hale telescope and by Low and G. Rieke at the University of Arizona, have shown that the apparently unitary core of the galactic nucleus is in fact made up of *at least four separate sources,* each with different relative intensities at different wavelengths. At present,

---

[27] G. Neugebauer & Eric E. Becklin, "The Brightest Infrared Sources," *Scientific American,* April 1973, page 28.

we lack the information needed to understand the sources unambiguously . . . the radiation could result from some non-thermal process [that is, some process different from a typical hydrogen fusion star] . . . Whatever the source of the infrared radiation, it may serve as a nearby example of processes taking place in the nuclei of other galaxies. Such nuclei exhibit a variety of phenomena, some of which are shared by the nucleus of our own galaxy. Specifically, many galactic nuclei show evidence for strong non-thermal radiation at both visible and radio wavelengths, and in a number of them, one can observe outflows of gas and other signs of violent activity. At radio wavelengths, the center of our galaxy also shows strong non-thermal emission and outflow. A number of galaxies exhibit radiation at 20 microns well in excess of that expected from ordinary stars . . . The amount of power such galaxies radiate in the infrared corresponds to as much as 10 times the power output of the sun. This is approximately the amount of power radiated by all the stars in our galaxy at all wavelengths . . . Enough has already been observed to indicate that the center of our galaxy is far from quiescent . . . By far the brightest object at 100 microns is the complex of sources associated in the nucleus of the [Milky Way] galaxy.[28]

The above is indeed an impressive description of our celestial home, and from a source altogether unexpected to throw light on a religious subject. It gives us some insight into what is meant when the Prophet Joseph said "God lives in everlasting burnings."[29]

GAMMA RADIATIONS

A study of gamma rays, radiating from several sites in our galaxy, is also enlightening. Dr. Leventhal of Bell Telephone Laboratories, et al, reports gamma rays from a great number of positions, detected by a balloon-carried instrument high over Australia. But they got the best results when they measured the Milky Way center. These experiments show there are "violent processes" at work in the nucleus of the Milky Way.

---

[28] Ibid., page 28-40.
[29] *Teachings of the Prophet Joseph Smith*, ibid, page 361.

For 17.3 hours, its telescope was aimed at the galactic core and detected gamma rays at the full range of observable wavelengths (energies) . . . The cores of some, and perhaps all galaxies, seem to be scenes of periodic explosions. Observations of the core of the Milky Way at wavelengths that penetrate the dust, such as those of radio and infrared emissions, indicate violent activity of some sort. Some theorists, such as Viktor Ambortsumian in the Soviet Union, have long argued that *processes unknown to physicists may be active in the galactic cores.* [Indeed, the light and power of God's throne!] . . . Sir Fred Hoyle and his associate, Jayout Vishnu Norlikar, have proposed that *matter is continuously created in the galaxy's core,* the matter being ejected but the antimatter remaining . . . The sheer amount of positrons [electrons with a positive charge, which occur in antimatter] observed toward the galactic center, . . . [suggest] the existence there of some sort of exotic object.[30]

PASS THROUGH THE VEIL

Earlier in the chapter, we mentioned that radio, infrared, and gamma radiation can pass through the veil of dust between earth and the center of the galaxy easier than visible light. Of course, Latter-day Saints know other ways to part the veil—faith, righteousness and prayer. At the end of the Millennium, the earth will pass through a veil and enter the celestial presence, as explained by Orson Pratt:

> By and by, when each of these creations [worlds] has fulfilled the measure and bounds set and the times given for its continuance in a temporal state, it and its inhabitants who are worthy will be made celestial and glorified together. Then, from that time henceforth and forever, there will be no intervening veil between God and His people who are sanctified and glorified, and He will not be under the necessity of withdrawing from one to go and visit another, because they will all be in His presence. It matters not how far in space these creations may be located from any special celestial kingdom where the Lord our God

---

[30] Walter Sullivan, "Balloon Data," *The New York Times,* April 27, 1978, page B10, emphasis added.

shall dwell. They will be able to see Him at all times. Why? Because it is only the fall, and the veil that has been shut down over this creation that keeps us from the presence of God. Let the veil be removed, which now hinders us from beholding the glory of God and the celestial kingdom, [and we shall be in His presence].[31]

CONCLUSION

The "light" and energy that emanates from the core of the galaxy is manifested in many of the electromagnetic spectra. All these radiations, and others we do not yet understand, confirm the statement from the Lord which says, " . . . the light which shineth, which giveth you light, is through him who enlighteneth your eyes . . . which light proceedeth forth from the presence of God to fill the immensity of space" (D&C 88:11–12). Earth is shielded from these radiations, in large measure, by a veil of dust. If not, the telestial earth would be incinerated.

---

[31] Orson Pratt, ibid.

Chapter 5

The Number of God's Creations

GOSPEL PRINCIPLES, THE BASIS OF THIS CHAPTER

God revealed to Moses that He had created "worlds without number" (Moses 1:33). Also "as one earth shall pass away . . . even so shall another come" (Moses 1:38). But the creation of worlds by God are but His secondary work. His primary focus and work is the progress of His children, for God said "this is my work and my glory to bring to pass the immortality and eternal life of man" (Moses 1:39). To accomplish this He has to build many suns and earths as mortal, temporary residences for His many children.

IS THE MILKY WAY TOO SMALL?

Some may feel the Milky Way Galaxy is too small a place to hold the dominions of our God. Let us examine the scriptures that define the scope of God's creations. In the Pearl of Great Price we read:

The words of God, which he spoke unto Moses . . . .

And, behold, thou art my son; wherefore look, and I will show thee the workmanship of mine hands; but not all, for my works are without end, and also my words, for they never cease.

Wherefore, no man can behold all my works, except he behold all my glory; and no man can behold all my glory, and afterwards remain in the flesh on the earth. [Moses 1:1, 4–5, emphasis added]

We can see less of our own galaxy, than any visible external galaxy. Our theory suggests we purposely are "curtained off," with veils of dust that prevent us from beholding all the creations of Heavenly Father and from beholding His blazing throne. Moses' interview with the Lord continues:

And worlds without number have I created; and I also created them for mine own purpose; and by the Son I created them, which is mine Only Begotten.

But only an account of this earth, and the inhabitants thereof, give I unto you. For behold, there are many worlds that have passed away by the word of my power. And there are many that now stand, and innumerable are they unto man; *but all things are numbered unto me, for they are mine and I know them.* [Moses 1:33, 35, emphasis added]

From Moses' discussion with the Lord, we learn that God's worlds are numbered unto him, and therefore their count is a finite number at that instant in time. This number is so large it cannot be numbered unto man. The Psalms remind us even though there are vast numbers of stars, God knows the number and the name of each one. "Praise ye the Lord . . . He telleth the number of the stars; he calleth them all by their names" (Psalms 147:1, 4). Once again, these statements are as true for our galaxy as they are for the universe, for man cannot number the suns or planets of either. They simply are too vast. Man's inability to number the worlds is not from being unable to express large finite numbers, but rather man could not count that high even in many lifetimes.

Like Moses, Enoch also had a vision with an accompanying in-terview with Deity. In worshiping God he said, "Were it possible that man could number the particles of the earth, yea millions of earths like this, it would not be a beginning to the number of thy creations" (Moses 7:30).

All the particles of millions of earths would be a large number indeed. We wonder if we could consider this statement by Enoch as a worshipful hyperbole.

A more accurate count of all of God's creations might be estimated in the minimum. The 150 billion stars estimated in our Father's Galaxy might each have several planets. Let's say three planets plus the sun (our sun has ten) giving a total of 150 billion x 4 = 600 billion creations. This number is beyond the comprehension of man, but to God each part is known and named. In this count we overlook all the moons, asteroids, and comets which must exist about each planet as they do about our's. If you count these, we have a huge number indeed.

We have found no scripture that refutes this idea of the Kolob Theorem, that God can count His worlds and suns, but man cannot. We believe every scripture describing God's creations would allow all of them to fit inside the great Milky Way system.

MEASURING VAST DISTANCES

The Kolob Theorem holds that the creations of Eloheim are contained within the limits of the Milky Way Galaxy. Our galaxy is a system of billions of stars and worlds so extensive that its vastness exceeds man's ability to comprehend. Measuring in units of miles is inadequate. If we use the circumference of the earth (25,000 miles), or the distance to the moon (250,000 miles), or the distance to the sun (89,000,000 miles) as yardsticks, the numbers still are far too large to comprehend. Astronomers have been forced to invent a new yardstick to permit some grasp of the extent of the heavens.

Light travels at the fastest speed of anything known to science—186,000 miles per second. In a year's time, light travels six trillion miles. This distance is known as one light-year. This is equivalent to 250 million earth circumferences.

The star nearest our sun is Alpha Centauri. Light from Alpha Centauri arrives after traveling for four years; therefore, it is said to be four light-years distant. Four light-years is much more convenient than saying 24,000,000,000,000 miles. The use of light-years helps with the expression of interstellar distances but not with the true comprehension of them. Can anyone actually grasp the twenty-four trillion miles? Consider the star Alderbaran, 60 light-years distant—fifteen times farther than Alpha Centauri. But these are only the nearby stars. Our galaxy is huge!

The earth is located 27,000 light-years from Kolob, which is in the bright core of our galaxy. Think of this vast distance. There are 162 quadrillion miles (162,000,000,000,000,000) between earth and Kolob! The radio and x-rays received on earth from the galactic center were emitted from the core 27,000 years ago. The earth is about 13,000 light-years from the outer edge of the galaxy. Thus, we are located about two-thirds of the galactic radius from the center, the galaxy being 80,000 light-years or 480,000,000,000,000,000 miles (480 quadrillion) in diameter.

Is there any man who can really grasp the cubic volume of our galaxy? The numbers are simply beyond comprehension. We only can state the numbers representing the totals without any real under-standing of each item in the total; let alone numbering and naming each creation as our Heavenly Father does. Therefore, there is enough room for God to create all the kingdoms or worlds He wants with space to spare within the Milky Way.

The observable system in the universe appears to be more and more galaxies, all receding from each other. Each galaxy appears largely independent from the others and controlling the movement of its own stars, just as would be predicted by the Kolob Theorem, which holds that each galaxy's core is the seat of a controlling deity.

GRAVITY—GOD'S LAW

For unnumbered eons, the stars of our galaxy have been circling Kolob. Gravity, the attractive force between one mass and another such as the central mass of the galaxy and its satellites (including our sun), was first described by Isaac Newton. This force is powerful and universal. It is one of God's vast powers. Gravity reaches to the most distant of His stars and locks it in an elliptical orbit about Kolob. Elder Orson Pratt said this power was one of God's laws. He said:

> When we undertake to investigate the laws which govern the various departments of nature, we are investigating the laws of God. Says one, 'Do you mean that the law of gravitation, which was discovered by Sir Isaac Newton, by which all bodies in the universe are held in their proper position, is a law of God?' Yes.[32]

The governing power of gravity must be one of God's priesthood powers by which He regulates and orders His dominion, for Abraham said there were great stars that were clustered near the throne of God, "And the Lord said unto me: These are the governing ones; and the name of the great one is Kolob, . . . I have set this one to govern all those [suns and worlds] which belong to the same order as that upon which thou standest" (Abraham 3:3). It appears this governing is done by gravity, one of God's laws.

ASTRONOMERS LEARN OF THE MILKY WAY GALAXY

Mankind has not always conceived of the heavens as we do today. Ptolemy held the earth was the center of the heavens. Copernicus followed with the notion that all creation was centered about the sun. Only in recent times has the present model of a galaxy been discovered and widely accepted. We can credit the American astronomer Harlow Shapley for his "eccentric" universe idea, first described in

---

[32] Orson Pratt, ibid.

A.D. 1925. His theory holds that the earth and sun are remote to the center of the galaxy, and the sun is proceeding in orbit about the galactic center.

Careful star counts per unit of space, even to the unaided eye, show a marked increase as you approach the Milky Way, which stretches across the night sky. A simple three-inch telescope will show three or four times the star density in the Milky Way as shown in a direction perpendicular to it. Using a 15-inch telescope, the ratio becomes nearly ten to one.

In addition to this visible increase in star density, the Milky Way also widens as you follow along its length until you come to the direction of Sagittarius, which is understood to be the center and the area of greatest stellar concentration. At first, the Milky Way was thought by astronomers to be a fuzzy region or luminous cloud and came to be called a "nebula," the Latin word for "cloud." Later astronomers discovered that what seemed to be fuzzy was actually a dense concentration of billions of stars.

Before Dr. Shapley's discovery in 1925, the widely held theory said our sun held the central position in our nebula and that our nebula contained all the stars in the universe. Both of these ideas are now known by science to be false. It comes as no surprise to Latter-day Saints to learn that 85 years before Dr. Shapley, Joseph Smith stated that the sun orbited Kolob (Abraham Facsimile 2:5), and therefore, could not be the center of the universe.

THE NUMBER OF STARS IN
THE MILKY WAY GALAXY

Inside our wheel-shaped galaxy there exists between 100 and 200 billion stars. This figure is an estimate, for no astronomer has counted them or ever seen them all. Many stand in the line of sight of a closer star, and many more are hidden behind veils of dust. Even if we could see them all, it would take 4,500 years to count them at a rate of one per second, 24 hours per day, 365 days per year. If you were Noah and had lived from the flood until the present, and used all your time counting, you would just now be completing the task. This number is only the stars, how many more worlds and moons are there? Well could the number of Heavenly Father's creations be described as "innumerable to man."

THE SPEED OF GALACTIC ROTATION

Our sun, carrying the earth, moon and all the solar system with it, is hurtling through space at a terrific rate of speed. The sun's orbital speed about the hub of the galaxy is 135 miles per second or 504,000 miles per hour (over one-half million miles an hour). The solar system is continuously pulled toward the center of the galaxy by gravity, and continually pulled away from the center by centrifugal force. These forces equalize themselves, thus locking the sun into an elliptical orbit about the galaxy's core. But we feel no movement. This traveling continues all day, all night, century after century. There is no evidence that the sun's movement about the galaxy has ever increased its speed or slackened its pace. The system does not run down or lose power or momentum. There is no indication that there is danger of our sun colliding with any of the other 150 billion stars which belong to this system and which also revolve about the galactic core. All this motion is in addition to the 65,500 miles per hour our earth circles about the sun. What supreme order and apparently effortless, perpetual motion. Could anything as elaborate and powerful be created by anyone but an all-wise God? Certainly, it did not create itself nor come by chance. Well did Jesus say concerning the heavens, "Behold, all these are kingdoms, and any man who hath seen any or the least of these [stars] hath seen God moving in His majesty and power" (D&C 88:47).

DYNAMIC GALACTIC ROTATION

The billions of suns in the Milky Way are each independent from each other (except for the binary stars). Each star has a separate orbit and speed about the heart of the galaxy. Table 1 shows data that illustrates the fluid nature of our galaxy. Stars at a distance of 5000 light-years from Kolob move at a velocity of 350,000 miles per hour. At this speed, it takes stars 56 million years to complete one galactic revolution. There is a different tangential velocity for each distance from the core of the galaxy. The speed increases to half a million miles per hour at a distance of 25,000 light-years from Kolob, then begins to slow down toward the outer edge of the galaxy.

TABLE 1

Tangential Velocities of Stars of the Milky Way Galaxy
and Length of the Galactic Year at
Various Distances from the Galactic Center[33]

	Distance From Galactic Center	Tangential Velocity	Number of Earth Years to Make one Galactic Rotation
	Light years	Miles per hour	Million earth years
Hub	?**	?**	?**
[Kolob]	5,000	350,000*	56*
	10,000	425,000*	89*
	15,000	493,000*	114*
	20,000	515,000	147
	25,000	500,000	188
Our Sun	27,000	481,000	200
	30,000	475,000	237
	35,000	439,000	301
Periphery	40,000	403,000	374

*Values uncertain
**While these movements in our galaxy are uncertain, radial velocities in galaxies with black holes have been measured using the Doppler effect, to be at an astonishing 957,000 miles per hour 25 light-years out from the center.

While the periphery makes one rotation of the galaxy, the stars of inner orbits make many annual turns. Our sun, for example, has

---

[33] Based on data from Bok & Bok, ibid.

completed 1.9 annual galactic rotations in the time the periphery completes one such rotation. Thus, the long arms of the spiral galaxies are trailing behind the tightly twisted central regions.

AGES OF THE STARS

Astronomers have measured the surface temperature, brightness, and color of local stars and find they vary greatly. It is possible to classify most of the stars according to these measurements along the "H-R diagram of the main sequence" of stars. The youngest stars appear as hot, blue-white stars, burning with surface temperatures of 50,000°F and radiating 10,000 times the energy as the sun. Our sun is midway along this aging sequence. It is an average star and burns with a surface temperature of about 40,000°F and is yellow in color. Older stars in the main sequence burn red in color and with a relatively cool temperature of 5000°F. There are also stars that do not fit into the main sequence. These stars include "white dwarfs" and "red giants."

The young blue-white stars are found mostly in the outer rings and arms of spiral galaxies, such as our Milky Way. The older stars in the main sequence are cool red stars that are found in the centers of spiral galaxies. These two facts are noteworthy: it appears young stars tend to appear in the telestial regions, while older stars are found in the center, the place of God's first creations.

CHRIST AS THE CREATOR, CHRIST FROM ETERNITY

The appreciation of our God and His Christ is greatly increased as we consider the vastness of His creations and the time it took Them to do it.

Our faith in Him, grows as we realize He came as the humble babe to Bethlehem and, as a man, walked this earth, one of the billions He made. Why this particular earth? He explained to Jacob and Enoch that this earth was the only planet whose inhabitants were wicked enough to put Him to death (2 Nephi 10:3; Moses 7:36). Yet, the Atonement He worked out for mankind on this earth is equally effective for all the worlds His hands have made.

Joseph Smith wrote a poem that was published in the Church newspaper, in Nauvoo, before the martyrdom. In the poem, Joseph restates his vision of the three degrees of glory:

> And I heard the great voice bearing record from heaven, He [Jesus] is the Savior and only begotten of God; By him, of him, through him the worlds were all made. Even all that career in the heavens so broad. *Whose inhabitants, too, from the first to the last, are saved by the same Savior as ours.* And of course are begotten God's daughters and sons, by the very same truths and the very same powers.[34]

This idea is reinforced by the Lord's simplified explanation of His visiting His twelve other, "kingdoms" or worlds one after another, likely during the millennial period of each. He said He will visit each one in succession and each one "will be made glad with the light of the countenance of his Lord" (D&C 88:51–57).

We understand this to mean Christ's Atonement is valid for all of Heavenly Father's worlds. Truly, what great glory the Savior possessed in the premortal world, and what great "condescension" (1 Nephi 11:16) He exercised to come as a man to this earth, to humble Himself and work out the wonders of the Atonement.

W.W. Phelps was such a close confidant of the Prophet Joseph Smith that he was asked by Joseph's family to preach at Joseph's funeral. Six months later, Brother Phelps wrote a letter to William Smith, the prophet's brother, to explain what was going on in Nauvoo. In this letter, published in the Church newspaper in 1845, Brother Phelps gives information apparently from the Prophet, but is published in no other source. Phelps shows that Christ, the Creator, has been about His Father's business for over two and a half billion years! He wrote:

---

[34] *Times and Seasons,* Aug 1843, Vol 4:4, emphasis added.

Well, now, Brother William, when the house of Israel begins to come into the glorious mysteries of the kingdom, and find Jesus Christ, whose going forth, as the prophets said, have been from of old, from eternity: and that eternity, agreeably to the records found in the catacombs of Egypt, has been going on in this system, (not this world) almost two thousand five hundred and fifty-five millions of years: . . . it almost tempts the flesh to fly to God, or muster faith like Enoch to be translated and see and know as we are seen and known![35]

An eternity, according to Brother Phelps, is two billion, five hundred, fifty-five million (2,555,000,000) years. Assuming these are earth years, we can convert them to God's time. Since there are 1000 earth years in a day to the Lord, (Abraham Facsimile 1:1) there would be 365,000 earth years in one of God's years. Therefore this two and one-half billion earth years expressed in God's years is a neat 7000!

$$\text{An eternity} = \frac{2{,}555{,}000{,}000 \; earth \; years}{365{,}000 \; \text{earth-years}} = 7{,}000 \text{ God years}$$

Latter-day Saints should be impressed with the above whole, round number; for 7,000 exactly matches in earth years the duration of the earth's temporal or probationary period (D&C 77:6). Likewise, 7,000 God years is the duration of an eternity. But saying He was from eternity (2.5 billion years ago) to eternity (perhaps another 2.5 billion years) gives us a way to understand Him better. Perhaps these numbers give us an exact meaning for the Savior coming in the "meridian" of time. (Moses 5:57) The term "elder brother" hardly tells the great antiquity of this "first born among many brethren"(Rom. 8:29). These facts should increase our love and admiration, if not astonishment, for Him, our Jehovah, the Lord Omnipotent.

---

[35] William W. Phelps, *Times and Seasons*, January 1, 1845, Vol 5, No. 24.

IS THERE A LIMIT TO THE NUMBER
OF GOD'S CREATIONS?

The Lord said to Enoch that He had created worlds without number (Moses 1:36). We should accept this statement from the point of view of men on this earth; it is to man that God's creations are beyond counting. The Prophet Joseph Smith taught there are other deities, also. He said there are Lords many and Gods many and that he was not "scared to death of such a doctrine" (*Teachings of the Prophet Joseph Smith,* p.373). These deities surely have creations and dominions comparable to our Heavenly Father's, and thus, there are some remote worlds, stars, and creations that are not of our Father's making.

However, in another sense, He is intimately tied and related to all the external Gods and galaxies of the global universe. Likely God is sealed by priesthood ordinances to His Fathers before Him, and they to their children, so that every galaxy with its presiding deity is probably linked in one vast eternal family of the Gods.

The Kolob Theorem may fly in the face of several cherished and widely held beliefs about our Heavenly Father and His works. Some may feel that it is blasphemous to teach that God is limited in any way. However, from man's point of view, Eloheim, our Father, is the Greatest, the Most Powerful, the Wisest, "and the extent of His doings none can find out" (D&C 76:2). He possesses these attributes in their fulness and perfection. For us, in all the generations of the gods, we believe there to be none wiser or more important than He is to us.

In stating that God's dominion is within the Milky Way Galaxy, we are declaring that God has created a finite (though extremely large) number of creations to date. The Kolob Theorem is not limiting the ultimate number of His creations or worlds. The galaxy appears to be in equilibrium. God said to Moses, "And as one earth shall pass away, and the heavens thereof even so shall another come; and there is no end to my works" (Moses 1:38). Perhaps the material of the galaxy is recycled and reused (see "Black Holes," page 16).

BOUNDS SET TO THE HEAVENS

The idea that there may be a boundary or a limit to God's works is hinted at in the revelation given to Joseph Smith at Liberty Jail:

> A time to come in the which nothing shall be withheld, whether there be one God, or many gods, they shall be manifest.
>
> All thrones and dominions, principalities and powers, shall be revealed and set forth upon all who have endured valiantly for the gospel of Jesus Christ.
>
> *And also, if there be bounds set to the heavens* or to the seas, or to the dry land, or to the sun, moon, or stars—
>
> All the times of their revolutions, all the appointed days, months, and years, and all the days of their days, months, and years, and all their glories, laws, and set times, shall be revealed in the days of the dispensation of the fulness of times—" [D&C 121:28–31; emphasis added]

CONCLUSION

We conclude the worlds created by our Heavenly Father are so many they cannot be numbered by man. However He knows each one. All of these could fit into the vast Milky Way Galaxy. It is gigantic in size, it is in rotary motion and moves with the power and majesty of God. We also conclude it may have taken not less than two and one-half billion years to build it.

Chapter 6

Location of the Three Degrees of Glory

COROLLARY 4:

LOCATION OF THE THREE DEGREES OF GLORY

The terrestrial and telestial kingdoms are located in successive concentric, doughnut-shaped rings, round about the celestial kingdom or central hub of the Milky Way galaxy; that our sun and earth are now located in the outer or telestial ring of the galaxy.

GOSPEL PRINCIPLES, THE BASIS OF THIS CHAPTER

There are three degrees of glory in the resurrection described in wonderful detail (D&C 76). We have already studied the celestial kingdom; here we consider the terrestrial and telestial kingdoms. Paul identified these glories in the resurrection as being similar to the sun, moon and stars. (1 Cor. 15:40–42). Each of these three places will be the final residence of a part of mankind after the judgment and the resurrection based on their works and faith while on earth. The location of these kingdoms of glory will be considered.

STRUCTURE OF GOD'S UNIVERSE

In 1832, while Joseph Smith and Sidney Rigdon were at work on the Joseph Smith Translation of the Bible, they asked the Lord the meaning of John 5:29, concerning the resurrection of the just and the unjust. The answer from the Lord is now recorded in Doctrine and

Covenants Section 76, as the vision of the three degrees of glory. This majestic document explains the structure of God's kingdoms, which previously were only vaguely hinted at by the Apostle Paul (1 Corinthians 15:40–41).

Ten months later, another revelation was given to the prophet, further expanding our understanding of these three kingdoms. This revelation is known as the "Olive Leaf, plucked from the Tree of Paradise" (D&C 88).

THE MILKY WAY GALAXY IN THE KOLOB THEOREM
DIVIDED INTO THE THREE DEGREES OF GLORY
PLUS OUTER DARKNESS

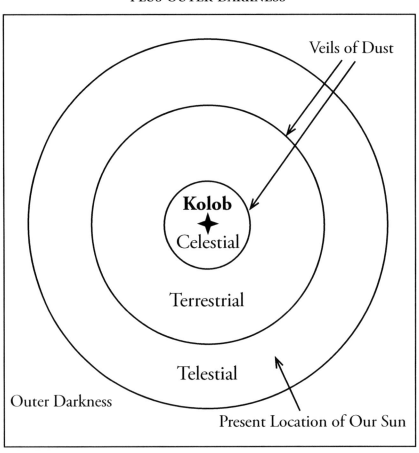

DESCRIPTION OF THE CELESTIAL KINGDOM

We were born in pre-earth life and lived with our Father in His celestial kingdom. After this earth life the saints expect to return to Him in the celestial kingdom. The Kolob Theorem holds that this place is in the fiery center of our Galaxy.

Those who come forth in the resurrection of the just will be pure and faithful and shall dwell in the presence of God and His Christ forever and ever. "These are they whose bodies are celestial, whose glory is that of the sun, even the glory of God, the highest of all, whose glory the sun of the firmament is written of as being typical" (D&C 76:70). This kingdom "excels in all things—where God, even the Father, reigns upon his throne . . . And he makes them [the righteous] equal in power, and in might, and in dominion" (D&C 76:92, 95).

The earth "must needs be sanctified from all unrighteousness, that it may be prepared for the celestial glory. For after it hath filled the measure of its creation, it [the earth] shall be crowned with glory even with the presence of God the Father" (D&C 88:18–19). Within "the celestial glory, there are three heavens or degrees; And in order to obtain the highest, a man must enter into this order of the priesthood [meaning the new and everlasting covenant of marriage]; And if he does not, he cannot obtain it. He may enter into the other, but that is the end of his kingdom" (D&C 131:1–4). These scriptures give us some understanding of God's home or the celestial kingdom.

THE CELESTIAL KINGDOM AS SEEN BY THE KOLOB THEOREM

The Kolob Theorem calls for divisions within the great Milky Way Galaxy, and, perhaps, all galaxies. In photographs of Andromeda Galaxy, the core appears brilliant white. The celestial zone has a thickness of about 16,000 light-years and perhaps, has a similar diameter. The shape of the celestial kingdom, therefore, might resemble a sphere. The celestial kingdom likely is located in this central bulge of the galaxy and consists of many millions of celestial orbs.

DESCRIPTION OF THE TERRESTRIAL KINGDOM
Then Joseph and Sidney

Saw the terrestrial world, and behold and lo, these are they who are of the terrestrial, whose glory differs from that of the church of the Firstborn, who have received of the fulness of the Father, even as that of the moon differs from the sun in the firmament.

. . . who died without the law;

. . . the honorable men of the earth, who were blinded by the craftiness of men.

. . . who receive of the presence of the Son, but not of the fulness of the Father.

. . . [whose] bodies are terrestrial

. . . who [are] not valiant in the testimony of Jesus. [D&C 76:71–72, 75, 77–79]

The terrestrial kingdom "excels in all things the glory of the telestial, even in glory, and in power, and in might, and in dominion" (D&C 76:91). "For he who is not able to abide the law of the celestial kingdom cannot abide a celestial glory . . . [and] must inherit another kingdom even that of a terrestrial kingdom" (D&C 88:21–22).

Also we understand that translated beings, the Garden of Eden and the Millennium are all of this Terrestrial order.

THE TERRESTRIAL KINGDOM AS
SEEN BY THE KOLOB THEOREM

The Kolob Theorem places the terrestrial kingdom in a dough-nut-shaped ring, concentric to the celestial core, with a shape thicker at the inside edge than the outside edge. In the color portrait of Andromeda this zone shines red in color (see page xiii).

In such a terrestrial zone, Christ and ministering angels visit the inhabitants of such worlds face-to-face. The earth during the Garden of Eden period and the Millennium is of this order. Heavenly Father visited Adam in the Garden of Eden via the principle that those in the

terrestrial kingdom may receive ministration from the celestial kingdom (D&C 76:87). The Kolob Theorem would also place Enoch's
Zion in this part of the galaxy.

Joseph Smith gave an explanation that translated beings are of a
terrestrial order and are prepared to be ministering angels:

> Many may have supposed that the doctrine of translation was a
> doctrine whereby men were taken immediately into the presence of
> God, and into an eternal fulness, but this is a mistaken idea. Their
> place of habitation is that of terrestrial order, . . . for such charac-
> ters . . . [are] held in reserve to be ministering angels unto many plan-
> ets and . . . as yet have not entered into so great a fulness as those who
> are resurrected from the dead.[36]

President Joseph Fielding Smith spoke concerning the terrestrial
zone as follows:

> Those who have lived a terrestrial law will be assigned to a terres-
> trial kingdom on some other globe. Those who have lived a telestial
> law will have to go to a telestial sphere suited for their condition.
> Where these worlds are, the Lord has not revealed to us, however, there
> are spheres now being prepared for them.[37]

It would appear there are two types of terrestrial worlds: First,
there are temporary ones, like the City of Enoch, or the earth in the
Garden of Eden period and during the Millennium. Secondly, there
must be some permanent terrestrial planets suitable for the eternal
home of those who inherit that glory in all eternity.

Certainly many of the suns that compose the terrestrial ring of
the galaxy have planets and moons orbiting them. Perhaps one of
these terrestrial planets is prepared or in the process of preparation to
receive the sons and daughters of earth, each in single status, who

---

[36] Franklin D. Richards and James A. Little, *Compendium of the Doctrines of the Gospel,*
Salt Lake City, Deseret Book Company, 1925, page 272.

[37] Joseph Fielding Smith, *Man: His Origin and Destiny,* 1954, page 539.

have kept only a terrestrial law. These will soon rise in a resurrection of terrestrial glory and find an eternal "dominion" awaiting them shining only with the luster of the moon. These shall be servants of the Most High. By our theorem their habitation is remote from Kolob, and they are isolated by a veil from their former celestial home. They remain so throughout all eternity for where God and Christ dwell they cannot come.

DESCRIPTION OF THE TELESTIAL KINGDOM

A vision of the third kingdom was then shown to Joseph and Sidney:

> We saw the glory of the telestial, which glory is of the lesser, even as the glory of the stars differs from the glory of the moon . . . .
>
> These are they who are thrust down to hell [temporarily].
>
> Who shall not be redeemed from the devil until the last resurrection. [D&C 76:81, 84–85]
>
> [Who] received not the gospel, neither the testimony of Jesus, neither the prophets . . . .
>
> These are they who are liars, and sorcerers, and adulterers and whoremongers. [D&C 76:101, 103]
>
> The inhabitants of the telestial world . . . [are] as innumerable as the stars in the firmament of heaven, or as the sand upon the seashore;
>
> For they shall be judged according to their works, and every man shall receive according to his own works, his own dominion, in the mansions which are prepared.
>
> And they shall be servants of the Most High; but where God and Christ dwell they cannot come, worlds without end. [D&C 76:109, 111–112]

The telestial kingdom receives the ministrations of the Holy Ghost and ministering angels from the terrestrial kingdom. The glory of the telestial "surpasses all understanding" (D&C 76:89). "He who cannot abide the law of a terrestrial kingdom cannot abide a terrestrial glory . . . [and] must inherit . . . [the] telestial kingdom" (D&C 88:23).

THE TELESTIAL KINGDOM AS SEEN BY THE KOLOB THEOREM

The telestial region of the galaxy is a donut-shaped ring concentric to the terrestrial kingdom. The telestial kingdom is thicker at its inside regions than at its outer edge. In Andromeda, this area shows faint blue in color.

The telestial kingdom is the present location of the earth. In due time, the earth will leave this region of the galaxy for a higher kingdom. Like the terrestrial zone, which contained two types of worlds, so also must the telestial kingdom contain two types of inhabited planets. Planets of the first type are only temporarily located here like the earth while in a mortal probation. Those of the second type are permanent telestial worlds for the children of Heavenly Father who inherit that kingdom forever.

CONCLUSION

When we observe an external galaxy we see it can be divided into three areas, each glowing with a different color of light. The Kolob Theorem identifies the center bulge of every galaxy as the location of a celestial kingdom, with outer rings successively as terrestrial and telestial kingdoms. Lanes of dust or veils we see in many galaxies may mark the boundaries between these kingdoms of glory.

Chapter 7

Location of Outer Darkness Place of Lucifer's Final Banishment

---

COROLLARY 5:
LOCATION OF OUTER DARKNESS

"Outer Darkness," the place of Satan's final banishment (D&C 76:44–49) with the sons of perdition, is beyond the reaches of the Milky Way Galaxy, where there is no light or heat, no suns or stars.

GOSPEL PRINCIPLES, THE BASIS OF THIS CHAPTER

The scriptures state that after the day of judgment, the devil, his angels, and those who "deny the Son after the Father has revealed him," will be banished to "outer darkness where there is weeping, wailing, and gnashing of teeth" (D&C 101:91).

They shall go away into everlasting punishment, which is endless punishment, which is eternal punishment, to reign with the devil and his angels in eternity, where their worm dieth not, and the fire is not quenched, which is their torment—

And the end thereof . . . nor their torment, no man knows;

Neither was it revealed, neither is, neither will be revealed unto man, except to them who are made partakers thereof;

Nevertheless, I, the Lord, show it by vision unto many, but straightway shut it up again;

Wherefore, the end, the width, the height, the depth, and the misery thereof, they understand not, neither any man except those who are ordained unto this condemnation. [D&C 76:44–48]

This is the place where those who suffer the "second death" shall go (D&C 76:37). This is a kingdom without glory, they are the sons of perdition.

THE OUTER DARKNESS AS SEEN BY
THE KOLOB THEOREM

At the outer edge of the Milky Way Galaxy lies a veil of dust, beyond which lies "outer darkness." An outer ring of dust of this type can be seen in an external galaxy (see Sombrero Galaxy, page xvi). Outer darkness is not simply intergalactic space. The sons of perdition are resurrected beings, possessing bodies of flesh and bone. With Satan, they will dwell in a real kingdom, an actual place—a planet. Nephi confirms the actuality of hell (1 Nephi 15:35). We do not know if there is one or more such planets of darkness. We believe them to be located beyond the outer limits of the galaxy. Such a planet would not orbit an active star and would be completely without light. Conditions there will approach absolute zero temperature and darkness possibly broken only by distant starlight. Whether these planets remain just outside the galaxy (but still orbiting about Kolob), or are "cast out" into true intergalactic space, we cannot even guess.

This picture of permanent Hell as a cold, dark world is completely at odds to the common idea of Hell as a place of fire and smoke.

CONCLUSION

Outer darkness, a kingdom without glory, must be located outside any of the kingdoms of glory for all of them shine and are lit up. We postulate the Devil and sons of perdition are cast out beyond the galaxy and shielded from it by a veil of dust.

Chapter 8

The Sequence of Earth's Development

COROLLARY 6:

SEQUENCE OF EARTH'S DEVELOPMENT

Our planet earth was first formed in an orbit of Kolob in the celestial core of the galaxy. It migrated out through the terrestrial ring (the Garden of Eden period), and took up its present position in an orbit of the sun, for its mortal, telestial probation. The earth will return by being pulled away from the sun, passing again through the terrestrial ring (the Millennial period), and finally regaining its original glorious orbit about Kolob in the celestial kingdom.

GOSPEL PRINCIPLES,
THE BASIS OF THIS CHAPTER

The earth is alive and changes from time to time. The earth has a spirit for it was created spiritually before it became temporal. It was clothed with spiritual vegetation and animal life. Animals also have spirits (D&C 77:2, Moses 2:30). Next, the earth became a Garden of Eden (Moses 3:8). After the fall of Adam, the earth became cursed or telestial, a fit place for mortal man (Moses 4:23–25). The Prophet Enoch, seventh from Adam, records he actually heard the earth speak, saying, "I [the earth] am pained . . . because of the wickedness of my children" (Moses 7:48). The earth also asked to be able to rest (Moses 7:48). This prayer of the earth will be answered after the second coming during the thousand year Millennium, a period of rest (Moses 7:64).

The Lord explained "the earth abideth the law of a celestial kingdom, for it fillith the measure of its creation, and transgresseth not the law . . . notwithstanding it shall die, it shall be quickened again" (D&C 88:25–26).

The Lord has also told us of the earth's final status:

> Therefore, [the earth] must needs be sanctified from all unrighteousness, that it may be prepared for the celestial glory;
>
> For after it hath filled the measure of its creation, it shall be crowned with glory, even with the presence of God the Father;
>
> That bodies [of men and women] who are in the celestial kingdom may possess it forever and ever. [D&C 88:18–20]

Some people believe in a static, inert earth unchanged for millions of years. But we advocate a living, changing earth progressing step by step towards its destiny in the celestial kingdom.

Only Latter-day Saints have this intimate view of our mother earth. Its journey to return to God is much like a human soul which advances through similar steps.

THE EARTH MAY BE SIMILAR TO A HUMAN SOUL

The scriptures outline to us that the earth had a spiritual creation, then a mortal creation; that the earth itself can talk, feel pain, and desire rest (Moses 7:48–49); that it is keeping a celestial law and in due time will die, be resurrected and celestialized (D&C 88:25). It is possible to show that the earth was baptized with water during Noah's flood and will be baptized later with fire at the second coming of Christ. In these several steps, it appears the earth follows a similar progression as a human soul.

The Lord explained the creation:

> For by the power of my Spirit created I them; yea *all things both spiritual and temporal—*

First spiritual, secondly temporal, which is the beginning of my work; and again first temporal, and secondly spiritual, which is the last of my work. [D&C 29:31–32, emphasis added]

For I the Lord God, created all things, of which I have spoken, spiritually, before they were naturally upon the face of the earth . . . for in heaven created I them. [Moses 3:5]

Only after all this, came the temporal creation of both the earth and mankind:

I, the Lord God, formed man from the dust of the ground, and breathed into his nostrils the breath of life; and man became a living soul, the first flesh upon the earth, the first man also; nevertheless, all things were before created; but spiritually were they created and made according to my word. [Moses 3:7]

The earth will apparently go through at least five steps of progression:

1. A spiritual creation occurred "in heaven" in the celestial core of the galaxy.

2. The earth was clothed with a physical body and when all things were ready, the earth passed through a veil and entered the terrestrial kingdom. Here earth as well as Adam and Eve experienced an innocent Garden of Eden period.

3. By the time of the fall, the earth had completed its transit of the terrestrial kingdom. Earth then passed through another veil into the telestial kingdom where it was captured by the gravity of the sun, about which the earth would revolve for 6,000 years of temporal existence.

4. Just before the second coming of Christ, the earth will leave its orbit about the sun, causing great physical upheavals, and pass through the veil into the terrestrial region. The earth and its people will then meet the Lord and enjoy a thousand years of paradisiacal glory.

5. After the earth has traversed the terrestrial zone of the galaxy, a thousand years, the earth will pass through another veil into the

celestial kingdom. The earth will be celestialized and changed into a great Urim and Thummim and receive a celestial glory. It will resume its former orbit about Kolob in the celestial core of the galaxy thus fulfilling the restoration of all things. It will remain in this position for evermore.

We will now present the scriptures and LDS sources which discuss each stage of the earth's development as interpreted by the Kolob Theorem.

EARTH CREATED NEAR KOLOB AND MOVES THROUGH THE TERRESTRIAL AND TELESTIAL

Brigham Young, who was instructed about astronomy by Joseph Smith, gives the following statement:

> When the earth was framed and brought into existence and man was placed upon it, it was near the throne of our Father in Heaven. And when man fell . . . the earth fell into space, and took up its abode in this planetary system, and the sun became our light . . . This is the glory the earth came from, and when it is glorified it will return again unto the presence of the Father.[38]

President John Taylor, who had also been taught by the Prophet, said the earth "had fled and fallen from where it was organized, near the planet Kolob."[39] These statements give us a clearer understanding of the term "in heaven," as used in the book of Moses: "For I the Lord God created all things . . . for in heaven created I them" (Moses 3:5). "In heaven" must mean near Kolob.

The remote place of the earth's origin is also disclosed in Abraham's account, "I saw that it [the earth at the start of the Garden of Eden Period] was after the time of Kolob, for as yet the Gods had not appointed unto Adam his reckoning" (Abraham 5:13). That is, the earth had not yet taken up its annual revolution about the sun.

---

[38] Brigham Young, *Journal of Discourses*, 17:143.
[39] John Taylor, *The Mormon*, August 29, 1857.

Mankind was also created in heaven.

The Kolob Theorem holds that there is celestial, terrestrial, and telestial matter, and that an orb in any of these kingdoms takes on the elements of its environment. When a planet moves to a higher kingdom, it burns off or discards the matter belonging to the previous kingdom and becomes like the kingdom it is entering.

The earth was created spiritually in the celestial core of the galaxy. As the earth passed through the veil, it took on terrestrial matter. This process constitutes the physical birth of the earth. At our personal birth, we also pass through the veil from heaven into a pure and innocent childhood state and acquire a physical body. At eight years of age, we as children, make another major change. We become accountable for our decisions and actions like moving into a telestial environment.

We suspect that when the earth fell from paradise to its mortal state, it passed through another veil into the telestial kingdom. As it entered this veil, it partook of telestial elements and became a telestial or mortal world subject to death. In reverse sequence, as the earth passes from the telestial to the terrestrial glory at Christ's second coming, it will shed telestial matter at the veil and be purified to a terrestrial level. Likewise, at the end of the Millennium, the earth will leave its terrestrial matter at the veil as it enters the presence of the Father as a bright, shining celestial orb.

EARTH FORMED FROM PARTS
OF OTHER PLANETS

Joseph Smith explained "this earth was organized or formed out of other planets which were broken up and remodeled and made into the one on which we live."[40] Perhaps this is the meaning of the scripture, "as one earth shall pass away . . . even so shall another come" (Moses 1:38).

---

[40] Richards and Little, ibid, page 287.

Elder James E. Talmage, speaking as a member of the Twelve and as a scientist, explained fragments of other planets were tiny spots of dust, not large blocks:

> The words of the Prophet have been construed as meaning that great masses of material have come together in space to form this planet, and that the broken and disturbed state of the earth's crust is an immediate result of these masses falling together in a disorderly way . . . . But the assumption that this broken condition of the crust blocks results from such blocks having been tumbled and piled together in the process of world-making, lying now *as they originally fell, is completely disproved by existing facts. No crustal irregularity or break has yet been observed, the nature or cause of which is obscure; indeed, the relation of every block to its contiguous formations may be demonstrated beyond question.*[41]

Elder Orson Pratt spoke further on the process of reusing matter from one creation to another:

> We are not to suppose that these elements, before they were collected, were formed into solid masses of rocks, and other substances; and that these came rushing together—rocks being piled on rocks, breaking, crashing, and rendering into millions of fragments. But no doubt, through the operation of antecedent forces, there had been a complete disorganization or dissolution of the bodies composed of these elements, in their prior state of existence anterior to the foundation of the present globe; this being the case, the elements being separate and apart, and widely diffused, were in a condition to come together in a state of particles, instead of aggregate masses . . .

> How many thousand millions of times the elements of our globe have been organized and disorganized; or how many millions of shapes or forms the elements have been thrown into in their successive organizations and disorganizations; or how widely the particles have been diffused through boundless space; or of how many different worlds

[41] James E. Talmage, *Improvement Era*, 1904, 7:481-488.

these particles have, at one time and another, formed the component parts; or how long that system itself has formed a branch of our stellar heavens—is unknown to us mortals.[42]

DUST MATERIALS ACCUMULATE AT THE BOUNDARIES

If this part of the Kolob Theorem is true, one would expect that at the interface of each kingdom of glory with another, there would be an accumulation of such "antecedent" matter; first being added to every entering globe and later left behind by each exiting globe. The boundaries are also the very places where the veils of dust are located. Likely the dust materials are, in fact, constituent parts of the veil.

That there are materials in space with which to clothe the earth in its physical tabernacle is clearly indicated in Abraham 3:24 emphasis added, "We will go down, for there is space there, and *we will take of these materials,* and we will make an earth whereon these may dwell."

TERRESTRIAL—THE GARDEN OF EDEN PERIOD
(See diagram on page 50.)

How long did it take for the earth to traverse the terrestrial zone of the galaxy, the time between the placing of Adam in the garden until his fall? Some clue is obtained from the fact that the opposite journey during the Millennium will take 1,000 years. Orson Pratt felt that the Garden of Eden period was indeed a similar 1,000-year period.[43] The Kolob Theorem holds that the Garden of Eden period probably lasted 1,000 years also. If the above statement is correct, we have reason for increased respect for Adam and Eve, who succeeded in resisting Lucifer for almost a thousand years. Lucifer and his angels lost the war in heaven and were cast down to the mortal earth. The

---

[42] Orson Pratt, *Formation of the Earth*, Elder's Journal, 3:161-164.
[43] Orson Pratt, *Journal of Discourses*, Vol 16, page 317.

scriptures indicate that Lucifer was present in the Garden of Eden. The devil and his forces must have been riding along with the earth, along with Adam and Eve, to the telestial kingdom as the earth was passing through the terrestrial zone of the galaxy.

EARTH BECOMES MORTAL

Brigham Young declared, "When man [Adam] fell, the earth fell into space, and took up its abode in this planetary system, and the sun became our light."[44] This idea was current in Nauvoo in the days of the Prophet Joseph, because one of the main articles in the Church newspaper said that at the fall, "the earth no longer retained its standing in the presence of Jehovah; but was hurled into the immensity of space; and there to remain till it has filled up the time of its bondage to sin and to Satan."[45]

The process of telestializing the earth likely included a cooling off period from the pleasant atmosphere enjoyed in the Garden of Eden. The terrestrial glory probably warmed Eden for 1000 years, and all the garden and its animals grew in profusion with no hint of bad weather. But the fall brought on the seasons through the lighting and heating of the earth by the radiations of the sun. The sun's warming by day is telestial. Consequently, there are now vast frozen regions at the earth's poles. Consider how Adam and Eve probably suffered during the transition to the telestial world which, of course, was a new and fearful experience for them.

EARTH TO BE PULLED AWAY FROM THE SUN, PASSES FROM TELESTIAL TO TERRESTRIAL

Eliza R. Snow, an acclaimed Latter-day Saint poet, was a wife of the Prophet Joseph Smith, and lived with him in Nauvoo. She was tutored by him in many gospel principles. We are indebted to her for

---

[44] Brigham Young, *Journal of Discourses,* Vol 17, page 143.
[45] *Times and Seasons,* Feb. 1, 1842, page 672.

composing 10 hymns now published in our current hymn book. In the 1891 edition of *LDS Hymns* appears a poem by Sister Snow, entitled "Hymn 322." Verses one through six and ten through twelve are reproduced below:

Thou, earth, wast once a glorious sphere
of noble magnitude,
And didst with majesty appear
Among the worlds of God

But thy dimensions have been torn
Asunder, piece by piece,
And each dismembered fragment borne
Abroad to distant space.

When Enoch could no longer stay
Amid corruption here,
Part of thyself was borne away
To form another sphere.

That portion where his city stood
He gained by right approved;
And nearer to the throne of God
His planet upward moved.

And when the Lord saw fit to hide
the "ten lost tribes" away,
Thou, earth, was severed to provide
The orb on which they stay.

And thus, from time to time, thy size
Has been diminished, till
Thou seemst the law of sacrifice
Created to fulfil.

When Satan's hosts are overcome,
The martyred, princely race

Will claim thee, their celestial home—
Their royal dwelling place.

A "restitution" yet must come,
That will to thee restore,
By that grand law of worlds, thy sum
Of matter heretofore.

And thou, O earth will leave the track
Thou hast been doomed to trace;
The Gods with shouts will bring thee back
To fill thy native place.[46]

We consider the phrase, "And thou, O earth will leave the track thou hast been doomed to trace," to mean the earth will leave its orbit about the sun in which it has been locked for its mortal probation. Also mentioned in the above poem is Enoch's Zion, which graphically demonstrates it is possible for matter to be taken from this solar system and moved to a higher kingdom: "Behold mine abode forever . . . and the Holy Ghost fell on many and they were caught up by the powers of heaven into Zion" (Moses 7:27).

Scriptural evidences that the earth may indeed be moved out of the solar system include:

1. "The earth shall remove out of her place" (Isaiah 13:13).

2. "If he say unto the earth—Move—it is moved" (Helaman 12:13).

3. "The earth shall reel to and fro like a drunkard, and shall be removed like a cottage" (Isaiah 24:20).

EVENTS ACCOMPANYING CHRIST'S RETURN

The following are some, but not all, of the signs that shall accompany the Second Coming of Christ: "There shall be earthquakes also in diverse places and many desolations" (D&C 45:33).

---

[46] Eliza R. Snow, *LDS Hymns*, 1891, Hymn No. 322, emphasis added.

Consider the gigantic forces of gravity required to pull the earth from the sun's gravitational field. The earth has a molten center, and when the floating plates comprising the earth's crust slide and push against each other, it will result in the greatest earthquakes known to man. "The whole earth shall be in commotion" (D&C 45:26). "Men . . . shall not be able to stand" (D&C 88:89). "The earth . . . shall reel to and fro as a drunken man" (D&C 49:23). "The stars shall become exceedingly angry, and shall cast themselves down:" (D&C 88:87).

As the earth accelerates away from the sun, seas will heave themselves beyond their bounds and the earth will reel to and fro. Eventually, "the land of Jerusalem and the land of Zion shall be turned back to their own place, and the earth shall be like it was before it was divided" (D&C 133:24). Thus will be fulfilled many scriptures concerning the Second Coming of Christ.

Prominent in the events accompanying the return of the Lord, will be great "signs and wonders, for they shall be shown forth in the heavens above" (D&C 45:40). These heavenly signs include the return of the ten tribes, as Sister Eliza R. Snow says, "a restitution yet must come, that to thee [earth] restore, by that grand law of worlds, thy sum of matter heretofore." Perhaps such a return is what the Prophet referred to when he declared, "Then will appear one grand sign of the Son of Man in heaven. But what will the world do? They will say it is a planet, a comet."[47]

Return of the Ten Tribes

According to Sister Snow, the ten lost tribes will make a dramatic return to the earth. The Doctrine and Covenants says when the ten tribes appear in the north countries, "They shall smite the rocks, and the ice shall flow down at their presence. And an highway shall be cast up in the midst of the great deep" (D&C 133:26–27). What could

---

[47] Richards & Little, ibid, page 275.

better melt the ice and shake the earth than a planet set down in the north countries carrying the lost ten tribes? There are other opinions related to the return of the ten tribes.

Elder Parley P. Pratt, writing in the Church's British newspaper, *Millennial Star*, told how all these returning fragments would greatly enlarge the size of the earth:

> The stars which will fall to the earth are fragments, which have been broken off from the earth from time to time, in the mighty convulsions of nature. Some in the days of Enoch, some perhaps, in the days of Peleg, some with the ten tribes, and some at the crucifixion of the Messiah. These all must be restored again at the 'times of the restitution of all things.' This will restore the ten tribes of Israel; and also bring again Zion, even Enoch's city. It will bring back the tree of life, which is in the midst of the paradise of God; that you and I may partake of it (see Revelation 2:7). When these fragments (some of which are vastly larger than the present earth) are brought back and joined to this earth, it will cause a convulsion of nature. The graves of the Saints will be opened, and they will rise from the dead. The mountains will flow down, the valleys rise, the sea retires to its own place, the islands and continents will be removed, and the earth will be many times larger than it is now. If I have told you of earthly things and ye believed not, how should ye believe if I tell you heavenly things? [John 3:12][48]

Darkness: The Sun and Stars Shall Refuse Their Light (D&C 34:9) Before the Coming of Christ

> The sun shall hide his face, and shall refuse to give light; and the moon shall be bathed in blood; and the stars shall become exceedingly angry, and shall cast themselves down as a fig that falleth from off a fig-tree. [D&C 88:87]

> But before that great day shall come, the sun shall be darkened . . . and the stars shall refuse their shining, and some shall fall, and great destructions await the wicked. [D&C 34:9]

---

[48] Parley P. Pratt, *Millennial Star*, Feb. 1841, Vol 1, No. 10, page 258.

The light of the sun will dim as the earth leaves the solar system. As earth begins to enter the dust which constitutes the veil, the perceived light of the sun and stars will be further darkened and eventually cease. Consider the terrible events in 3rd Nephi, which occurred prior to the Savior's visitation to the Nephites. The 3rd Nephi account is a type or shadow of the Second Coming: great earthquakes, seas heave themselves beyond their bounds, rough places made smooth, valleys exalted, the sun and stars refuse their light, and the wicked destroyed. All these destructions lead to the personal appearance of the Savior, following which the people who survive live together in paradisiacal harmony. Likely, as it was with the Nephites, so shall be the coming of the Son of Man.

Christ's Coming Occurs as the Earth Passes Through the Veil

It is completely consistent with Latter-day Saint theology that just as it passes through the veil, the earth will meet the Lord. As it is with men, so it is with the spherical earth: each must pass through the veil into the presence of the Lord.

The Lord will not come unaccompanied when He returns. "Then shalt thou [Enoch] and all thy city meet them there, and we will receive them into our bosom" (Moses 7:63). Enoch's Zion has already been translated into the terrestrial region of the galaxy. Earth may rendezvous with the City of Holiness at the veil, at the Second Coming of Christ.

When the Lord returns, "every corruptible thing, both of man, or of the beasts . . . or of the fowls . . . or of the fish . . . that dwells upon all the face of the earth, *shall be consumed; And also that [every corruptible thing] of element shall melt with fervent heat;* and all things shall become new" (D&C 101:24–25, emphasis added). Surely, the telestial elements will be consumed at His coming and will be left at the veil. Perhaps all the elements of the earth will be consumed, and the earth will be quickened with a terrestrial tabernacle. Such a shedding of the earth's old "body" and the putting on of a terrestrial one would be the equivalent of death and resurrection. Such an idea may be hinted at in the many scriptures which say that the earth will "pass away" (see Matt. 24:35; 2 Peter 3:10; 3 Nephi 26:3; D&C 29:23; Revelation 21:1; 1 Nephi 17:46; Alma 9:2–3; Ether 13:8; Moses 1:35, 38). In the Doctrine and Covenants we read concerning the earth, *notwithstanding it shall die, it shall be quickened [made alive] again and shall abide the power by which it is quickened*" (D&C 88:26, emphasis added).

CHRIST TO LIGHT THE EARTH, NO NIGHT THERE

The Apostle John described his vision of the Millennium as follows:

> I saw a new heaven and a new earth: for the first heaven and the first earth were passed away;

> And he carried me away in the spirit to a great and high mountain, and shewed me that great city, the holy Jerusalem [Enoch's Zion] descending out of heaven from God . . .

> And *the city had no need for the sun,* neither of the moon, to shine in it: for the glory of God did lighten it and the *Lamb is the light thereof. . .*

> *for there shall be no night there* (Revelation 21:1, 10, 23, 25 emphasis added).

Isaiah declares: "The sun shall be no more thy light by day; neither for brightness shall the moon give light unto thee, but the Lord shall be thy everlasting light, and thy God thy glory" (Isaiah 60:19).

Similarly, the Psalmist sang of the time when the "night shineth as the day" (Psalms 139:12).

The brilliance of Christ's coming to the earth will be sufficient to cover the earth, for the Prophet Joseph corrected the Bible text to say, "for as the light of the morning cometh out of the east and shineth even to the west and covereth the whole earth, so shall also the coming of the Son of Man be" (JS—Matt. 1:26, Matt 24:27).

During the Millennium, Christ's glory and light will shine from east to west and be seen by all men, "for His glory shall be upon them" (D&C 45:59). There will be no night during the Millennium. So mild and constant will be the weather during this time that apparently, the seasons will be eliminated, for Amos says, "the plowman shall overtake the reaper" (Amos 9:13).

During the 1,000 years of the Millennium, the earth will be in and traversing through the terrestrial zone. Each happy citizen of earth will be made "glad with the light of the countenance of his Lord" (D&C 88:56). Christ's glorious reign on earth is consistent with the pattern that says the Father ministers in the celestial, the Son in the terrestrial (millennial region), and the Holy Ghost in the telestial kingdom (D&C 76:86–87).

The scriptures state that at both the beginning and end of the Millennium, a drastic change will take place, wherein there will be a "new heaven and a new earth" (Isaiah 65:17; 2 Peter 3:13; Ether 13:9; Revelation 21:1). The earth will be changed to paradisiacal glory at the beginning of the Millennium and to celestial glory at the end. It is easy to understand why there will be a "new earth" on each of these two occasions.

EARTH PASSES FROM TERRESTRIAL TO CELESTIAL GLORY

When the 1,000 years of paradise has expired, and Lucifer is released and finally banished forever, the earth will "be rolled back into the presence of God and crowned with celestial glory."[49] As promised by the Lord, "after [the earth] hath filled the measure of its creation, it shall be crowned with glory, even with the presence of God the Father" (D&C 88:19). Sister Snow records, "The Gods with shouts

---

[49] Richards and Little, ibid, page 288.

will bring thee [earth] back to fill thy native place." Brigham Young adds that the purified and sanctified earth will be "placed in the cluster of the celestial kingdoms."[50]

According to the Kolob Theorem, at the end of the Millennium, the earth will pass from the terrestrial kingdom, through a veil of dust, into the celestial glory. Earth will once again be consumed by fire and changed into a fiery, celestial sphere.

> And the end shall come, and the heaven and the earth shall be consumed and pass away, and there shall be a new heaven and a new earth.

> For all old things shall pass away, and all things shall become new, even the heaven and the earth and all the fulness thereof, both men and beasts, the fowls of the air and the fishes of the sea. [D&C 29:23–24]

EARTH TO BE A GREAT URIM AND THUMMIM

The celestial earth will shine by itself. As Brigham Young taught, "When it becomes celestialized, it will become like the sun, and be prepared for the habitation of the Saints and be brought back into the presence of the Father and the Son. It will not then be an opaque body as it now is, but it will be like the stars of the firmament."[51] Orson Pratt adds that this earth will be classed "among the dazzling orbs."[52] Joseph Smith taught, "this earth in its sanctified and immortal state, will be made like unto crystal and will be a Urim and Thummim to all the inhabitants who dwell thereon" (D&C 130:9). Joseph's description of the celestial earth parallels St. John's description of the sanctified Zion: "And the street of the city was pure gold, as it were transparent glass" (Revelation 21:21). The earth "Must needs be sanctified from all unrighteousness, that it may be prepared for the celestial glory; For after it hath filled the measure of its creation, it shall be

---

[50] Brigham Young, *Journal of Discourses,* Vol 17 page 117.
[51] Ibid., Vol 7, page 163.
[52] Orson Pratt, *Millennial Star,* 12:72.

crowned with glory, even with the presence of God the Father; That bodies who are of the celestial kingdom may possess it forever and ever " (D&C 88:18–20).

CONCLUSION

Many scriptures attest to the earth being alive, created spiritually and moving step by step towards its final destination. It will become one of the shining orbs close to God's holy throne. The convulsions of nature to accompany Christ's second coming can best be understood by considering the trauma of earth leaving its orbit around the sun.

Chapter 9

Other Mortal Worlds within Our Milky Way

COROLLARY 7:

OTHER MORTAL WORLDS WITHIN THE MILKY WAY

Heavenly Father has many other worlds which follow the same pattern as earth and now exist in one of several stages of this progression; that many are now in their mortal period and are peopled with beings who look, act, and associate together as we do, for they also, are children of Heavenly Father.

GOSPEL PRINCIPLES, THE BASIS OF THIS CHAPTER

God's offspring are placed on other worlds as well as this earth (D&C 76:24, 88:51–57). Christ assisted the Father in the creation of all these worlds. Also Christ is the Savior and Redeemer of all of these other worlds. The Prophet taught us that the inhabitants of other worlds are "saved by the same Savior as ours."

OTHER CIVILIZATIONS WITHIN THE GALAXY

In recent years, much has been published on the scientific likelihood of many worlds existing in the universe which may sustain life and produce a civilization capable of interstellar communication.

All the physical elements found in our world are common to what is widely dispersed throughout the cosmos. There is nothing particularly unique about the structure of earth and its association with the sun that would preclude similar worlds about other stars. The same nuclear, chemical and physical laws known to us on earth have been demonstrated to work in the remote parts of the solar system.

Professor Hallis R. Johnson, of Indiana University, lists the pre-requisites for life as we know it, to exist in space. His list, based on carbon chemistry, includes water in a liquid state, a supply of oxygen, light, heat and adequate gravity.[53] He feels that it is not likely that life based on some exotic (non-carbon) chemistry exists. He reports factors considered by a group of scientists in West Virginia in 1961. These scientists met to consider the probability of communicating civilizations existing within the Milky Way. The factors, as determined by these scientists, are as follows:

A. What is the rate of star formation in the Milky Way Galaxy? He estimates it at 10 stars per year. Stars must be thought of as each being a sun.

B. What fraction of the stars have planets? Conservatively, he estimates one in ten. In another study, reported by Dr. Harrison Brown, of the 100 nearest stars to our sun, eight are known to have dark, invisible bodies associated with them by their "wobble," and 60 may have objects the mass of Mars or larger about them.[54]

C. How many planets are the correct distance from their sun for a life-supporting environment? He concludes that each remote solar system would, on the average, contain one such ideally located planet and be large enough to retain an oxygen atmosphere by its own gravity and has liquid water.

D. What chances are there that life will appear on such a favorable planet? Dr. Johnson concludes one in ten.

E. What chance is there that such life would produce a civilization? Again, he estimates one in ten.

---

[53] Hollis R. Johnson, "Civilizations Out in Space," *BYU Studies*, Autumn 1970, Vol. 11, No. 1, page 5.
[54] Hal Knight, "Are There Millions of Earth-like Planets?," *Deseret News*, Feb. 2, 1966, page A13.

F. Finally, he considers how many of these civilizations are communicative and for how long.

His final summary is that if a communicating civilization would last 1,000 years, there could be at least 100 such civilizations in our galaxy, and if such civilizations last a billion years, there would be 100 million such civilizations. "It seems very likely there are many civilizations in the [Milky Way] galaxy around us."[55]

TECHNOLOGY IS OF THE LORD

Consider the technical progress man has made in our lifetime. If we could continue such physical progress for a hundred or thousand more years, what a fantastic material world it would be!

Indeed, we consider it highly likely that the Millennium will be an era of extremely advanced technology. Children attending school, college students and professors will likely be asked to continue their endeavors after Christ's coming. The destructions that accompany Christ's return will likely destroy much of our industrial base, but as we have seen with Japan and Germany after World War II, this can be a chance to rebuild with the most advanced technology then available. Consider the primary work of the Millennium—temple work. This work is currently heavily dependent upon computers, audiovisual equipment, and temples that use electricity. If we, who are currently progressing at a snail's pace in this work, are dependent upon such technology, might not the Lord choose to use the same tools to advance and coordinate the millennial work among thousands of temples and billions of ordinances? It is hard to imagine linking the entire "book of the generations of Adam," with pencil and paper alone. These new technical inventions are from the Lord, and we suspect He will have His faithful Saints use them, even in the Millennium.

---

[55] Ibid., page 9.

LOCATING ALIEN CIVILIZATIONS

Some preliminary attempts have been made to find radio signals from civilizations inside the galaxy. There has been no real success thus far. In 1981, the US government funding of the project was canceled, but private funding by the Planetary Society of Pasadena, California, continued the search with sensitive new machines.

Professor Horowitz, a physicist and electronics expert, has proposed a sophisticated radio receiver to search for a type of signal that an alien society might be transmitting to Earth. The receiver will be able to listen to a quarter of a million radio channels simultaneously, will be attached to existing radio telescopes, such as the giant 1,000-foot antenna in Arecibo, Puerto Rico, and will look for signals at special or "magic" radio frequencies. These are frequencies, like TV channels, that would be known to other civilizations as well as ours, because the laws of nature are likely everywhere the same. Since these channels are distinctive, any signal in them would stand out from the random radio noise of the galaxy, and some scientists think that alien civilizations might use them to send announcements of their existence to newly emerging civilizations such as ours.

The idea of other worlds with intelligent beings on them may seem alarming to the average man, who concluded in the early centuries that the world and man were the center of the universe. However, to Latter-day Saints, all this has been long anticipated in the teachings of the gospel through the Prophet Joseph Smith.

MANY WORLDS

We have reason to believe that the number of inhabited worlds is larger than science has estimated. In the estimate previously cited, the scientist estimated that in worlds ideally suited for the development of life, few would actually produce life and civilization. However, if God were setting up these "ideal" settings, He would not fail.

In a great vision of the heavens, Moses was shown "worlds without number" which the Lord God had created. The Lord said:

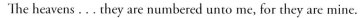

The heavens . . . they are numbered unto me, for they are mine.

And as one earth shall pass away and the heavens thereof, even so shall another come; there is no end to my works:

For behold, this is my work and my glory—to bring to pass the immortality and eternal life of man. [Moses 1:37–39]

Only an account of this earth, and the inhabitants thereof, give I unto you. For behold there are many worlds that have passed away by the word of my power. And there are many that now stand, and innumerable are they unto man; but all things are numbered unto me, for they are mine and I know them. [Moses 1:35]

These considerations lead to the conclusion that there must be many millions of life-sustaining worlds in our galaxy. Indeed, in Joseph's *Egyptian Alphabet and Grammar*, he refers to the "degree of light—cheering the face of millions of planets."[56] Latter-day Saints believe in many populated worlds.

WHAT DO THE INHABITANTS OF OTHER WORLDS LOOK LIKE?

According to the Kolob Theorem, life forms on other planets include the actual begotten children of Eloheim. The Lord revealed to Joseph Smith "That by him, [Christ] and through him, and of him, the worlds are and were created, and the inhabitants thereof are begotten sons and daughters unto God" (D&C 76:24). Note that "the worlds" have "inhabitants" and those inhabitants are children of our God.

Much good humor has been generated over a contemplation of little green men with horns existing on Mars or elsewhere in the universe. One author speculated on someday meeting a "green-bearded, triple-bellied" inhabitant of outer space. Latter-day Saints know such beings will look like men on earth. Since such inhabitants of other planets are sons and daughters of God, they also will be created in His image and likeness, male and female.

---

[56] Joseph Smith, *Egyptian Alphabet and Grammar,* page 28.

THE SAME LAWS OPERATE
ON OTHER WORLDS

The Prophet Joseph's statement that those of other worlds are saved by the very same Savior as ours[57] indicates that there are many planets following the same pattern as earth. Salvation through the Atonement of Jesus Christ is probably available to them on the same basis as it is to us. Such conditions must include keeping all the commandments, overcoming a devil (or devils) on their world, being baptized by water and Spirit, living a righteous life and receiving a priesthood sealing in marriage. God's priesthood knows no limit within His universe. Abraham gave us a picture of "God sitting on His throne, *revealing through the heavens* the grand key words of the priesthood" (Abraham Facsimile 2:7, emphasis added).

Jesus elaborated further on the extent of His kingdoms to Joseph Smith, "And there are many kingdoms; for there is no space in which there is no kingdom; and there is no kingdom in which there is no space, either a greater or lesser kingdom" (D&C 88:37).

Later, in the same revelation, the Lord explains He visits each of His creations in sequence:

I will liken these kingdoms unto a man [God] having a field [His galaxy], and he sent forth his servants into the field to dig the field.

And he said unto the first: Go and labor in the field, and in the first hour I will come unto you, [in your world] and ye shall behold the joy of my countenance.

And he said unto the second: Go ye also into the field, and in the second hour I will visit you with the joy of my countenance.

And also unto the third, saying: I will visit you.

And unto the fourth, and so on unto the twelfth.

And thus they all received the light of the countenance of their lord, every man in his hour, and in his time and in his season—

Every man in his own order . . . .

[57] Joseph Smith, *Times and Seasons,* August 1843, Vol 4:4.

Therefore, unto this parable I will liken all these kingdoms and the inhabitants thereof—every kingdom in its hour, [millennium] and in its time, and in its season, even according to the decree which God hath made. [D&C 88:51–55, 58, 60, 61]

Elder B.H. Roberts felt the pattern of presiding councils, consisting of presidencies and quorums, also exists on other worlds. He said, "Each Presidency of a system of worlds or of a single planet being the embodiment of that authority which extends all along the line of the Gods throughout the universe."[58] Based on God's words to Enoch, we conclude that the inhabitants of other worlds also experience wickedness and righteousness. He said, "I can stretch forth mine hands and hold all the creations which I have made; and my eye can pierce them also, and among all the workmanship of mine hands there has not been so great wickedness as among thy brethren" (Moses 7:36).

The Kolob Theorem holds that the mortality experience we find here on earth is being repeated many, many times within the galaxy. Indeed, it is a universal pattern for many previous worlds and many worlds yet to come.

MANY EXALTED WORLDS

If worlds beyond man's ability to number have followed the pattern of creation, Garden of Eden, mortality, millennium, and celestialization, we would expect to find many worlds have now finished their course and are exalted in the fiery core of the galaxy. No doubt, if we could see through the veil of dust into the galactic nucleus, we would be looking at many exalted worlds. Orson Pratt explains his view in these words: "When each of God's creations has fulfilled the measure and bounds set and the times given for its continuance in a temporal state, it and its inhabitants who are worthy will be made celestial and glorified together."[59]

---

[58] B.H. Roberts, "The Gods and Their Government," *Contributor,* 9:115-118.
[59] Orson Pratt, *Journal of Discourses,* 17:332-333.

CONCLUSION

We conclude from the evidence above that Christ created all the worlds of Heavenly Father. His Atonement wrought on this earth is valid and effective on all other worlds. The inhabitants of these other worlds look and act as we do for they are also children of God working out their mortal probation and that there are many worlds inhabited by Heavenly Father's other children.

Chapter 10

Counting Speed and Time

COROLLARY 8:

SPEED OF TRANSPORTATION

There must exist a speed of transportation of heavenly beings, faster than the speed of light, a speed such as the speed of thought.

COROLLARY 9:

COUNTING TIME

Heavenly Father has a system of time—a clock, shall we say, similar to ours but ticking more slowly; in ratio as one is to 360,000. Earth time is experienced only during the telestial probation of the earth. In addition, a terrestrial "clock" must exist to measure the time in the Garden of Eden and the Millennium periods.

GOSPEL PRINCIPLES,
THE BASIS OF THIS CHAPTER

God manages His kingdom efficiently. He has a very fast means of communications and transportation.

Travel between various places in God's kingdom can be done by spiritual beings at or near the speed of thought.

Time on earth (24 hours/day and 365 days/year) started with the fall of Adam (Abraham 5:13) and will end at the start of the Millennium (D&C 84:100). God's time passes much slower than mans'.

THE SPEED OF CELESTIAL TRANSPORTATION

Brother W.W. Phelps' poem, "If You Could Hie to Kolob,"[60] gives us an idea of instantaneous travel: "If you could hie to Kolob in the twinkling of and eye and then continue onward with that same speed to fly . . . " This speed, according to the Kolob Theorem, is 27,000 light-years in the twinkling of an eye. Such speed is, of course, unknown to science. The fastest speed of any form of matter or energy is the speed of light, 186,000 miles/second. The journey to Kolob at the speed of light would take 27,000 earth years. But we have many examples that such a trip has occurred in a small fraction of that time. Our Savior told His Hebrew apostles after the resurrection, that He ascended to His God and their God (John 20:17). Then, after having done so, He soon came down from His Father with commandments for the Nephites (3 Nephi 9:15). Thus, the Savior made a round trip from earth to Kolob and back. It takes light 54,000 years to make the same round trip journey. There must be a speed for heavenly or spirit objects to travel faster than anything now known to man. Moroni made a similar round-trip journey between A.D. 421 and A.D.1823. Or consider each newborn baby, newly arrived from the presence of God. Not one of us would hold that each baby would spend 27,000 years, at light speed, to get to its mother here on earth for birth.

Prayers are said, heard in heaven, and answered sometimes instantaneously. Frequently God answers us even while we are still asking the question in prayer. How could such messages travel back and forth with such speed? Science should be looking for travel speeds of incredible magnitude.

Elder Melvin J. Ballard expressed the idea that the three Nephites could move with the speed of thought. He said "they had power over the elements of earth, power over the law of gravitation, by which they could move over the face of the earth, in the *speed of their own thoughts.*"[61]

---

[60] Hymns of the Church of Jesus Christ of Latter-day Saints, hymn 284.
[61] Melvin J. Ballard, "The Path to Celestial Happiness," *Deseret News,* Oct. 31, 1925.

Brigham Young spoke concerning other worlds saying, "Worlds will continue to be made, formed and organized, and messengers from this earth will be sent to others . . . We shall make our home here [on the celestialized earth], and go on our missions as we do now, but at a greater-than-railroad speed."[62] What profound understatement, that such inter-world messengers would travel faster than a railroad train!

Another illustration of this principle is the angel Gabriel who was "caused to fly swiftly". While the Prophet Daniel was praying, God commanded the angel to fly to earth and give him a message. When he arrived, Daniel was yet praying and the angel had to touch him to get his attention (Daniel 9:19–23). The entire journey of Gabriel from the presence of God to Daniel on the earth took place in less time than Daniel's prayer. He must have traveled at the speed of thought.

GOD'S TIME AND MAN'S TIME

It may be difficult to believe that God has a clock, but apparently He does. In fact each globe or planet has its own way to count time. The Lord told Abraham through the Urim and Thummim, "Thus there shall be the reckoning of time of one planet above another, until thou shalt come nigh unto Kolob . . . it is given unto thee to know the set time of all the stars" (Abraham 3:9–10).

The Prophet Joseph made this explanation about different systems of time. "In answer to the question—Is not *the reckoning of God's time, angel's time, prophet's time and man's time according to the planet on which they reside? I answer yes* . . . angels do not reside on a planet like this earth; But they reside in the *presence of God, on a globe* like a sea of glass and fire" (D&C 130:4–7, emphasis added).

However the scriptures only give details on God's time and earth's time.

GOD'S TIME

Abraham confirms that God has His own system of counting time; it is based on the revolutions of Kolob.

> Kolob was after the manner of the Lord, according to its times and seasons in the revolutions thereof; that one revolution was a day unto the Lord, after his manner of reckoning, it being one thousand years according to the time appointed unto that [earth] whereon thou standest. This is the *reckoning of the Lord's time,* according to the reckoning of Kolob (Abraham 3:4, emphasis added).

The exact formula to calculate the ratio of God's time (celestial time) to man's time on the earth is given in Facsimile No. 2: "The measurement according to celestial time . . . One day in Kolob is equal to a thousand years according to the measurement of this earth" (Abraham, Facsimile 2:1).

Here we are comparing days with years. To make this understandable we must change the days to years so we can compare years to years. There are 365 days to a year. By multiplying 365 to each side of the equation we have; one year of God's time is 365,000 years of earth time or in ratio, as one is to 365,000.

This would mean the 7000 years of the earth's temporal existence (D&C 77:12) would be seven days of God's time or one week.

It becomes clear, then that the counting of time is real, calculable and understandable. But God's time runs very slowly compared to our earth.

Since we know God's time is the same as Kolob's, we have a way to understand the timing in the heart of the Milky Way Galaxy.

TERRESTRIAL TIME CHANGED
TO TELESTIAL TIME

We expect suns and planets have their own time systems. We should also expect a planet's timing to be changed if it would move from terrestrial to telestial as happened to earth, at the time of Adam's fall. Consider what we know of the counting of time in the Garden of Eden. In this case it seems the Lord's time was being used: "But of the tree of knowledge of good and evil thou shalt not eat of it; for in the time that thou eatest thereof, thou shalt surely die. Now I, Abraham, saw that it was after the *Lord's time*, which was after the time of Kolob; for as yet the Gods had not appointed unto Adam his reckoning" (Abraham 5:13).

As a point of verification, please note the "day" Adam partook of the fruit would not end without Adam dying first. At Adam's fall he received his reckoning of time and started counting his own age, we see he lived 930 years and died. (Genesis 5:5). The "day" in which Adam was to die was one of God's days since it was spoken of in the Garden of Eden, *1000 years on earth.* Adam's death was 70 earth years before this "day" expired.

TIME NO LONGER

Speaking of the time of the second coming of Christ, the Lord promises "Satan is bound and [earth] time is no longer" (D&C 84:100). Also at the sounding of the seventh trump ". . . there shall be time no longer; and Satan shall be bound" (D&C 88:110). We understand these scriptures mean *earth* time is no longer, for of course God's time, Kolob's time continues.

EARTH TIME TO LAST ONLY
SIX THOUSAND YEARS

Man's time or earth time nowadays we recognize as 24 hours/day and 365 days/year. It was after Adam's fall when earth time was established (Abraham 5:13). Probably this happened at the time the earth exited the terrestrial zone (Garden of Eden) and was captured in its orbit about the sun. It was only then the sun shown on earth in the day time as it rotated on its axis each 24 hours. Also it was only then the earth took a full 365 days to cycle through the four seasons and make one complete annual orbit about the sun.

The earth is continuing its temporal existence six thousand years until the start of the Millennium (D&C 77:7–12). At this time, the earth will end its telestial existence and start its terrestrial period. Earth time will end at the time when Christ will return to bind Satan and rule on earth (D&C 84:100) for the Millennium. We postulate the ending of earth time means the start of terrestrial time. This is the time earth draws away from the sun and will loose its means of counting time and will then need a new time system.

Also Alma's comment (Alma 40:8, emphasis added) "time only is measured unto man" does not mean no one else but man, has a clock. For in the same verse Alma says "all is as one *day* with God," or God counts days too. Apparently there are many different counting systems in the galaxy (Abraham 3:9).

The Kolob Theorem would identify the terrestrial system of time, will be appointed to men on earth at the second coming. This is the time when the earth draws away from the sun. This cancels "time" as we know it. The terrestrial system of time would continue for earth through the "day" of the Millennium, the thousand earth years when the earth is resting.

GOD SEES THE PAST AND FUTURE
WITH NO TIME LAG

The Lord has declared, "all things . . . are manifest past, present, and future, and are continually before the Lord" (D&C 130:7). Imagine living on a great Urim and Thummim like where God lives. Here is portrayed all things past, present, and future before him. On earth, we can only see the present; but God has the power to see forward or backward in time, as well as in space! He can see backward or forward in time the same way we may look to the right or left. Such powers are beyond the limits of our comprehension but are part of God's great powers. This understanding increases our admiration of him.

CONCLUSION

From the above chapter we see there are many systems of keeping time, but we have details on only two: one for this earth while it continues to revolve around the sun and the other for Kolob or God's time.

We can also conclude angels and spiritual beings can travel throughout the galaxy at the speed of thought.

Chapter 11

In Heaven's Image

COROLLARY 10:

In Heaven's Image

Things on this earth are patterned after, or even descended from, heavenly originals, and we can understand heaven in part by studying this earth. God Himself lives in a real place composed of actual materials on a crystal sphere—a great Urim and Thummim.

GOSPEL PRINCIPLES, THE BASIS OF THIS CHAPTER

Things on the temporal earth look like their counterparts which are spiritual, which God has created in heaven (D&C 77:2). The earth, all vegetation and animal life as well as mankind were first created in heaven as spirits (Moses 3:5) then created on the earth. Man was created on the earth in the image of God (Geneses 1:27). Thus we can better understand spiritual and heavenly things by observing things on the earth, for the earth is in heaven's image and likeness.

GOD IS TANGIBLE

It is a common doctrine among some churches that God is "so large that he fills the universe, yet so small he can dwell in your heart." Such a being is, of course, incomprehensible. Jesus said, "And this is life eternal, that they might know thee, the only true God, and Jesus Christ, whom thou hast sent" (John 17:3). Latter-day Saints worship a God who can be understood with the aid of the Holy Ghost. In fact, it is only by coming to know God and Christ that one may have eternal lives.

God is real, when our eyes are opened we will realize He is tangible and under the right circumstances we can feel Him and talk to Him.

The following scriptures speak plainly and eloquently concerning the actual and tangible nature of our Father in Heaven and His Son Jesus Christ:

- The Father has a body of flesh and bones as tangible as man's; the Son also; but the Holy Ghost has not a body of flesh and bones, but is a personage of Spirit (D&C 130:22).

- When the Savior shall appear, we shall see Him as He is. We shall see that He is a man like ourselves (1 John 3:2 and D&C 130:1).

- There is no such thing as immaterial matter. All spirit is matter, but it is more fine or pure, and can only be discerned by purer eyes; We cannot see it; but when our bodies are purified, we shall see that it is all matter (D&C 131:7–8).

HEAVEN IS A REAL PLACE
AND OCCUPIES "SPACE"

"And there are many kingdoms; for there is no space in which there is no kingdom; and there is no kingdom in which there is no space, either a greater or lesser kingdom" (D&C 88:37). This concept is important to the Kolob Theorem. It helps us realize we are talking about real places, which occupy space, even though we can't see them at present. Spiritual matter is so fine or pure (D&C 131:7) we cannot see it as mortals.

EARTH PATTERNED AFTER HEAVEN

While there are some differences, the Earth is much like heaven in several ways:

- Both heaven, as understood as God's throne, and the earth, are spherical in shape. God's throne is a "globe" (D&C 130:7). Similarly the earth is also a sphere.

- Both heaven, God's throne, and earth revolve about a sun; God's throne about Kolob and the earth about the sun. They are both planets thus inhabitants of each place can walk on the surface where they live.

- The inhabitants of each place can "talk" to each other just as we do here.

- There is vegetation and animals in each place.

- Under the right circumstances husbands and wives can form a family and have children, spirit children in heaven who become mortal children on an earth.

- However, there are differences:
    All things in Heaven are perfect but not so here.
    We are subject to sin and death on the earth.
    Also mortals on earth sleep, but spirits do not sleep.

President Heber C. Kimball wrote the following to his children, "Everything we see here is typical of what will be hereafter."[63] The Lord said to the Prophet Joseph, "That which is spiritual being in the likeness of that which is temporal; and that which is temporal in the likeness of that which is spiritual" (D&C 77:2). It appears that earth life was patterned after our pre-mortal existence, and our post-mortal life will be patterned after our earth life.

The family structure (D&C 131:1–4), some form of Church organization (D&C 76:54), possession of homes or mansions (John 14:2), possession of land and property (D&C 45:58), usage of books (Revelation 20:12), and many other parallels appear to exist between our celestial home and our present existence.

---

[63] Heber C. Kimball, *Masterpieces of LDS Leaders,* N.B. Lundwall, page131.

TALKING, VISITING AND BEING SOCIAL

Many people have noted the close bond—the brotherhood and sisterhood—felt between and among family members, church members and close friends. Spirituality is not found by withdrawing from society, but by stretching one's soul in service to others. The brotherhood and sisterhood we should enjoy in the church here will continue into the next life. Our beloved Prophet Joseph Smith wrote, "That same sociality which exists among us here will exist among us [in heaven], only it will be coupled with eternal glory, which glory we do not now enjoy" (D&C 130:2).

We can easily visualize how the spirit world is for the saints from the words of Brigham Young: "Spirits sleep not . . . Spirits walk, talk, hold meetings, have no illness, move like lightning, enjoy life and the society of the just, the righteous and not be subject to the devil."[64]

All this allows us to think in concrete terms about spirits, other worlds and Kolob.

The best scripture we have to teach us that our bodies on earth look like our pre-earth spiritual bodies is found in the Book of Mormon. In this case the Brother of Jared, about 2600 B.C., took sixteen transparent stones he had moltened out of the rock to the Lord and asked Him to touch them so they would shine. Thus they would have light in their barges while crossing the ocean.

> The Lord stretched forth his hand and touched the stones one by one with his finger. And the veil was taken from off the eyes of the Brother of Jared, and he saw the finger of the Lord . . . .
>
> And the Lord said unto him; Because of thy faith thou hast seen that I shall take upon me flesh and blood . . . .
>
> Behold the Lord showed himself unto him and said . . .
>
> I am he who was prepared from the foundation of the world to redeem my people, Behold, I am Jesus Christ . . . .

---

[64] John A. Widtsoe, *Discourses of Brigham Young,* Deseret Book Company, 1977, page 380.

This body which ye now behold is the body of my spirit; and man have I created after the body of my spirit, and even as I appear unto thee to be in the spirit will I appear unto my people in the flesh" (Ether 3:6, 9, 13–14, 16).

On the basis of this account, we conclude our spirit bodies, in pre-earth life, look like our mortal physical bodies do in the flesh, just as Jesus' spirit looked like His earthly body.

Both man and beast appear to be patterned after and perhaps descended from heavenly originals. We are informed that Adam and Eve were created in the image of God (Genesis 1:27). God is the creator of Adam and Eve's physical bodies. He is also the Father of every man and woman's spirit. Thus, both spiritually and physically, we are descendants of our God. No wonder we look like him.

EDUCATION, SEEKING WISDOM

In our assemblies, we should edify one another and seek divine understanding and wisdom. This same pattern of learning appears to have existed in our pre-mortal life. Solomon wrote the following concerning wisdom in the former life:

The Lord possessed me in the beginning of his way, before his works of old.

I was set up from everlasting, from the beginning, or ever the earth was.

When there were no depths, I was brought forth; when there were no fountains abounding with water.

Before the mountains were settled, before the hills was I brought forth:

While as yet he had not made the earth, nor the fields, nor the highest part of the dust of the world.

When he prepared the heavens, I was there: when he set a compass upon the face of the depth:

When he established the clouds above: when he strengthened the fountains of the deep:

When he gave to the sea his decree, that the waters would not pass his commandment: when he appointed the foundations of the earth:

Then I was by him as one brought up with him: and I was daily his delight, rejoicing always before him;

Rejoicing in the habitable part of his earth; and my delights were with the sons of men. [Proverbs 8:22–31]

Nor will acquiring wisdom be finished in this life. Instruction and admonition continue in the next life. Joseph Smith said:

When you climb up a ladder, your must begin at the bottom, and ascend step by step, until you arrive at the top; and so it is with the principles of the gospel—you must begin with the first and go until you learn all the principles of exaltation. But it will be a great while after you have passed through the veil before you will have learned them. It is not all to be comprehended in this world: it will be a great work to *learn our salvation and exaltation even beyond the grave.*[65]

PROCREATION

The sacred procreative powers given to man and woman here on earth are in the image and likeness of those powers used by our heavenly parents to beget spirit children (D&C 132:19). This same privilege will be granted to the faithful, of this earth, in the resurrection, and thus, the pattern of generating new life will be continued for another generation of the gods.

THE PLANTS AND ANIMALS

Individual beasts, and plants appear to be patterned after their spirits, which were previously organized in heaven. An account of the creation of the spirits of all life that come upon the earth is contained in the Pearl of Great Price:

---

[65] Joseph Smith, Quoted in the *Contributor,* October 1882–September 1883, page 255-256, emphasis added.

And now, behold, I say unto you, that these are the generations of the heaven and of the earth, when they were created, in the day that I, the Lord God, made the heaven and the earth,

And *every plant of the field before it was in the earth, and every herb of the field before it grew.* For I, the Lord God, created all things of which I have spoken [he previously mentioned *creating fowls, fish, beasts,* plants, etc.], spiritually, before they were naturally upon the face of the earth . . . And I, the Lord God, had created all the children of men; and not yet a man to till the ground; for in heaven created I them. [Moses 3:4–5, emphasis added]

CONCLUSION

We can conclude from the above discussion that mortal earth and heaven are look-alikes; only the earth is temporary and dark and heaven is glorious, shining and constant. Not only man is tangible but our Father in Heaven and Jesus Christ, our Lord, are also tangible beings (D&C 130:22). This is true of heaven or of God's residence which is also real and tangible and exists in time and space. The earth is but a replication of a very ancient heavenly model or pattern.

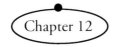

Chapter 12

Children of Heavenly Father Become Deities

COROLLARY 11:

CHILDREN OF HEAVENLY FATHER BECOME DEITIES

Faithful children of Heavenly Father who follow His celestial laws will have the opportunity, after their resurrection and exaltation in the celestial kingdom, to form new galaxies with Kolobs—each with a new hub, with suns and worlds as places of residence for their own countless spirit offspring giving rise to a new generation of the gods.

GOSPEL PRINCIPLES, THE BASIS OF THIS CHAPTER

God has promised "all he has" as an inheritance for His faithful children (D&C 84:38, 132:16–17, 29, 37). To receive all the Father has is to become a "god" (D&C 76:58). The plan of God's universe must anticipate matter and space for these new inheritances to be organized and given to all who become exalted in the highest heaven. This is the place where repentant and believing humans are going. We should be interested in this for it is our future home; a place of eternal families and eternal increase.

This idea is in sharp contrast of the current idea that Heaven is a blissful place, resting on billowy clouds, playing harps and only singing praises. We reject this idea as being without family, purpose, growth, achievement and quite stagnant.

FAITHFUL CHILDREN OF HEAVENLY FATHER CAN BECOME GODS

As the faithful children of Heavenly Father enter into their exaltation, there must be places or "mansions" prepared as the seats for these future deities. The Saints will receive an inheritance on our celestial earth. There will also be future Kolobs—future celestial centers with large stars of governing size—about which galaxies may be built and revolve. Our Theorem must allow for matter and space for these new emerging gods and their new galaxies.

As we all know the blessing of godhood, which we call exaltation is reserved for those precious saints who embrace the fulness of the gospel, repent of all sin, keep every commandment of God as taught by The Church of Jesus Christ of Latter-day Saints, believe in the merits of Jesus Christ as the Savior and Redeemer, are sealed to their spouse for eternity and with their spouse are finally sealed by the Holy Spirit of Promise. They must also continue and endure in faith unto the end of mortal life. After the resurrection, only to such is the crown of eternal lives and godhood awarded. All the rest remain as servants, separate and single through all eternity, in their saved condition, in a degree of glory according to their faith and works (D&C 132:16–17).

GLOBULAR CLUSTERS

The Kolob Theorem requires some place in the universe where new embryonic galaxies can be organized for faithful children of God who win the crown of exaltation. As one possible mechanism to accomplish this, we offer the "globular clusters." These are spherical in shape, move in orbits far above the plane of the Milky Way but revolve about our galactic center. They appear to be completely separate from the stars in the plane of the galaxy.

A mature galaxy has a glorious celestial hub and spiral arms which are divided into terrestrial and telestial portions. Another prominent feature of some spiral galaxies, at least our own, is the existence of globular clusters.

Globular clusters are highly concentrated, spherically shaped systems of stars. Globular clusters contain from about ten thousand to one million stars and have an average diameter of about 100 light-years. The Globular Cluster 47 Tucanae, shown here is an example of these magnificent structures. Globular clusters are located in equal number on either side of the galactic plane. Professor Harlow Shapley plotted the position of these bodies in space and determined they were evenly distributed revolving about a point in space beyond the Sagittarius constellation. This central point turns out to be the center of the Milky Way Galaxy or Kolob. Using the wide orbits of globular clusters, Professor Shapley was the first to determine the center of the galaxy.

Is this picture an embryonic galaxy?

Globular Cluster 47 Tucanae from SALT
South African Astronomical Society, http://antwrp.gsfc.
nasa.gov/apod/ap050905.html

Globular clusters are made of ancient type II stars, which are the same type of stars found in the celestial core of the galaxy. They also resemble the core of the galaxy in that the greatest star size and star concentration appear in the controlling center regions of the cluster. Astronomer Colin A. Ronan wrote, "It seems also, both from observations and from gravitation theory, that the stars in a cluster are not evenly distributed. The outer ones are probably a couple of light-years or so apart, whereas those near the center are separated by only a fraction of a light-year. The general opinion is that the stars near the center are tightly packed."[66] Such a description is reminiscent of Abraham's description of the regions near the throne of God. He said there are many "great ones" [stars] near Kolob. In this respect, and in star type, globular clusters resemble miniature or perhaps embryonic galactic hubs.

Globular clusters are not located within the dust-veiled plane of the galaxy. Instead, they orbit the core of the galaxy, in wide orbits, far above the plane of the galaxy.

There must be a mechanism by which new deities receive their own celestial kingdom and begin to create suns and worlds. The Kolob Theorem maintains globular clusters may be young celestial kingdoms inherited from Eloheim by those who have entered into exaltation. These individuals will need the space and materials to create galaxies of their own. The globular clusters perhaps could be moved out into space, away from the Milky Way Galaxy and grow to become a full grown Galaxies. But if this proves not to be true, where and how are new galaxies organized?

Could Jesus have reference to this process when He said to His Hebrew apostles, "In my Father's house are many mansions: if it were not so, I would have told you. *I go to prepare a place for you*" (John 14:2 emphasis added).

TWO PLACES OF GOVERNMENT

Some may ask, how could an exalted man and wife live in the center of a new galaxy when he is promised an inheritance on this earth when it is celestialized and close to Kolob? Could this be answered with the possibility that such a new deity could have two seats of government. The scriptures promise the Saints will inherit the earth, receive an eternal inheritance upon it, and dwell in the presence

---

[66] Colin A. Ronan, *Deep Space,* MacMillan Publishing Co., NY, 1982, page 58.

of God forever. In addition such exalted persons could also have a home in the center of a new Galaxy they are building.

Such a consideration leads one to ask, "Is the great sea of glass upon which Eloheim now resides, nigh to Kolob, be the same orb He used to live on when a mortal? Likely He may have two locations of government; one near to Kolob where He administers His own galaxy for His children (D&C 130:4–8); and the other, in the center of His Father's galaxy which He inherited from His father. Perhaps we too will have two locations.

Every exalted couple may eventually receive their own celestial globe which will be located at the center of their own galaxy. There, the righteous will create and populate worlds without number.

In addition, the righteous from this earth will also have an inheritance upon our earth, when it is celestialized.

Since both places are within the celestial kingdom, where instant communication is possible, the distance between them may not be a problem.

It likely takes a very long time to have enough spirit children to people a galaxy, or even a world. In this interim period, which may last eons, the celestial couples very well may live on our celestial earth in the heart of the Milky Way Galaxy. There, we may have sociality with God, Christ, and the righteous of this earth. Mormonism teaches that God delights in the association of friends and families. Regardless of the creation of new galaxies by those reaching Godhood, there will probably be many visits "home" to our Father and to our brethren.

CONCLUSION

From this chapter we conclude that God is able to fulfill His promises of exaltation to His children who live the fulness of His gospel. Apparently He is starting embryo galaxies (perhaps as globular clusters) for the faithful children to inherit. As we consider this future day of inheritance our faith in God greatly increases. We can see He is able to keep His word.

Chapter 13

Deities in Addition to Eloheim

COROLLARY 12:

DEITIES IN ADDITION TO ELOHEIM

The un-numbered billions of external galaxies beyond our Milky Way are not the creations of Eloheim, but each has its own deity, its own celestial kingdom in its fiery core, with terrestrial and telestial kingdoms round about. Perhaps galaxies, in turn, cluster and revolve about ever-higher centers.

GOSPEL PRINCIPLES, THE BASIS OF THIS CHAPTER

Our father Eloheim, had a father.[67] This revelation to the Prophet Joseph (although known before, Revelation 1:6), opens a window of understanding of the entire cosmos. Now we can visualize the whole picture; it stretches out before us as billions of galaxies. There is no end to them regardless of what direction we look. When we see these galaxies, external to the Milky Way, we realize that they are not the creations of Eloheim but likely of His forefathers and relatives who are gods also.

GODS BEFORE ELOHEIM

President Joseph Fielding Smith said, "Our Father in heaven, according to the Prophet Joseph, had a Father, and since there has

---

[67] Joseph Smith, *Teachings of the Prophet Joseph Smith,* ibid, page 373.

been a condition of this kind through all eternity, each Father had a Father."[68] Brigham Young explained that "there never was a time when there were not Gods and worlds and when men were not passing through the same ordeals that we are now passing through."[69]

If one ponders these statements, the conclusion is reached that there is a large number of gods. Indeed, the process by which the gods reproduce themselves is infinitely old and has no beginning. Even the number of generations of the gods is infinite. As we study the extended universe we should expect to find places where these deities have their kingdoms. Perhaps one of them is presided over by Eloheim's father and there may be found the old world, now exalted, where Eloheim lived as a mortal so long ago.

THE NUMBER OF GALAXIES

With the most powerful telescopes (two hundred-inch reflector and the NASA Hubble), scientists can see over 1,000 million galaxies (see Fred Hoyle, *Frontiers of Astronomy,* p.245). However, the theory of this book would require that if you were to travel untold light-years to the most distant galaxy which we now see and then look beyond you would see additional galaxies stretching out before you. There simply is no end to the number of galaxies.

Elder William W. Phelps' poem, "If You Could Hie to Kolob" (LDS Hymn, number 284), teaches this same profound lesson on Mormon cosmology:

If you could hie to Kolob in the twinkling of and eye,
And then continue onward With that same speed to fly,
Do you think that you could ever, Through all eternity,
Find out the generation Where Gods began to be?

Or see the grand beginning, where space did not extend?
Or view the last creation, Where Gods and matter end?

---

[68] Joseph Fielding Smith, *Doctrines of Salvation,* Vol 2, page 47.
[69] Brigham Young, *Deseret News,* 16 Nov. 1859, page 290.

Methinks the Spirit whispers, "No man hath found 'pure space,
Nor seen the outside curtains, Where nothing has a place."

The works of God continue, And worlds and lives abound;
Improvement and progression Have one eternal round.
There is no end to matter; There is no end to space;
There is no end to spirit; There is no end to race.

We postulate, according to the Kolob Theorem, that each of these many galaxies is governed by its own god who is striving to bring eternal lives to His offspring (see picture of many galaxies, page xvii).

GALACTIC CLUSTERS

Astronomer Colin A. Ronan has noted, "As telescopes, cameras and other equipment for probing deep space improve, and as new surveys of the sky are made, it is becoming clear to astronomers that isolated galaxies are unusual. They more commonly occur in pairs or in groups of three or more; our Local Group is no rarity but a typical example. As well as in small groups, galaxies are to be found in clusters, from a hundred or so up to thousands."[70] Likewise, Isaac Asimov wrote:

> There are hundreds of clusters of galaxies visible in the sky. They are obviously clusters because of the close proximity of the individual members in space and of the similar luminosity of the larger members. Some of the clusters are enormous. There is one cluster in the constellation Comma Berencies, about 120,000,000 light-years distant, that is made up of about 10,000 individual galaxies.[71]

The Kolob Theorem holds that the Milky Way Galaxy may be in a grand orbit about Eloheim's Father's galaxy, which in turn, is in orbit about the galaxy belonging to Eloheim's Father's Father, and so on, ad infinitum. We speculate the galactic clusters we observe in the heavens are a reflection of the patriarchal order among the Gods.

---

[70] Colin A Ronan, ibid, page 106.
[71] Isaac Asimov, ibid, page 195.

The above model of the universe wherein galaxies are grouped into clusters, which are grouped into super clusters and so forth, has been proposed by astronomer De Vaucouleurs as a "hierarchy universe."

Before leaving the subject at hand, we will discuss how the Kolob Theorem fits into current models of the extended universe. The two most widely discussed models of the universe are the Big Bang Theory and the Steady State Theory. The first is the most widely accepted of the two.

THE STEADY STATE OF THEORY

The Steady State universe can best be visualized as follows: Imagine a universe of infinite volume filled with an infinite number of galaxies that are evenly distributed in space. Now imagine that space itself is expanding. In such a mode, the universe would essentially look the same for all observers. No matter from which galaxy one observes, all external galaxies would be seen retreating. The more distant the galaxy, the greater the velocity at which it retreats. Such seems to be what astronomers observe when they look into distant space. In the space between the galaxies, we propose, there is room for new galaxies to grow.

Imagine that as the universe expands, matter is continuously being created from which new galaxies may be formed. Isaac Asimov (who is not a proponent of the Steady State Theory), described this theory as follows:

> But the requirements of continuous creation theory are small indeed; matter needs be created only at the rate of one atom of hydrogen per year in a billion liters of space, and such a rate of creation would be far too small to be detectable by any instruments we possess . . .
>
> As the galaxies recede from each other, whatever the cause, the spaces between gradually accumulate matter through continuous creation.
>
> The accumulation is slow, to be sure, but so is the rate at which galaxies recede from each other, compared to the vast spaces between.

It takes several eons [billions of years] for the distance between two neighboring galaxies to double, and by that time, enough matter has been formed between them to condense into a new galaxy.[72]

Brigham Young stated in the *Journal of Discourses*:

> We cannot receive, while in the flesh, the keys to form and fashion kingdoms and to organize matter, for they are beyond our capacity and calling, beyond this world. In the resurrection, men who have been faithful and diligent in all things in the flesh, have kept their first and second estates, and worthy to be crowned Gods, even the sons of God, *will be ordained to organize matter.* How much matter do you suppose there is between here and some of the fixed stars which we can see? Enough to frame many, very many millions of such earths as this, yet it is now so diffused, clear and pure, that we look through it and behold the stars. Yet the matter is there. Can you form any conception of this? Can you form any idea of the minuteness of matter?[73]

Under the Steady State Theory, the universe is not only generally the same for all observers in space, it is also the same for all observers in time. Indeed, the universe would never be born, for there is no beginning. It would never die, for "continuous creation" would allow it to be continually growing.

The Steady State Theory has lost followers among astronomers over the past several years because they feel observations of the most distant parts of the universe suggest that the universe looked differently in the distant past than it does now. Such findings are not undisputable, however, and scientists are not in agreement on the meaning of the data. (For further reading on both Steady State and Big Bang theories, see Isaac Asimov's *The Universe*, chapters 14, 15, and 19.)

The Steady State Theory is particularly appealing to Latter-day Saints because of our doctrine that there is no beginning or end to the generations of the gods. The continuous creation of matter out of

---

[72] Ibid., page 224.
[73] Brigham Young, *Journal of Discourses,* Vol 15, page 137, emphasis added.

nothing is impossible, since Joseph Smith wrote, "The elements are eternal." The elements were once thought to be the atoms which appear on the chemist's Periodic Table of the Elements. Atoms were thought to be indivisible and could neither be created or destroyed. We have since learned that atoms are not "elemental" but can be broken down into protons, neutrons, and electrons. These sub-atomic particles are also divisible. Matter can be converted into energy, and, under special situations, energy can be converted into matter. Could part of the enormous energy spewing out from the center of our galaxy be converted into matter to build new kingdoms, new galaxies?

We have limited understanding on how to produce new energy and new matter which must be available ad infinitem. Perhaps disbursed in the infinite volume of space are the pre-existing elements which could form new creations. Perhaps these elements have been there forever. This would be necessary to build new galaxies for emerging deities. Perhaps it could be based on recycling. We hold that there will be plenty of matter and space for the new kingdoms which God has promised.

THE BIG BANG THEORY

The Big Bang Theory states that all matter and energy in the entire universe was originally at one location. This mass exploded and sent matter and energy, of which the galaxies are composed, hurtling in all directions. Today, all galaxies outside our local cluster are receding from us, just as one would expect from such an initial explosion. Radio astronomers can also detect a background radiation in all directions, which scientists believe to be the remnant of such an initial explosion. If the initial explosion were great enough, the universe will expand forever, with the galaxies getting farther apart, until only those in our local cluster are visible. If the power of the initial explosion were small, or under a certain value, gravity will ultimately pull the universe back to a single lump of matter, destroying the worlds and galaxies as we know them. The cycle would then be repeated with yet another explosion and a new beginning.

CONCLUSION

The exalted relatives of Eloheim have and will organize worlds and suns and will govern and populate galaxies as did all the gods before them. This pattern will be continued throughout all eternity. There will always be enough matter and space to allow this growth.

Summary and Conclusions

Many gospel principles are considered in this book. The meaning of the scriptures describing these principles are greatly enhanced when we lay them out in sequence of the Kolob Theorem and compare them to recent discoveries from the science of astronomy which, in many cases, are catching up with what the prophets have said long ago. After due reflection on the data presented in this book, we list below the summary and conclusions we feel are probable or likely explanations of the structure of the universe.

CHAPTER 3
GOD'S THRONE AND KOLOB ARE LIKELY AT THE CENTER OF THE MILKY WAY GALAXY

Abraham saw, by the Urim and Thummim, the huge star Kolob, "that it was nearest to the throne of God" (Abraham 3:2); that Kolob is the first of all of God's creations and is the greatest (largest in mass) of all the stars (Abraham 3:16), and that it "governs all the stars which belong to the same order as that upon which thou [Abraham] standest [earth]" (Abraham 3:3). The scriptures also establish that God's throne is in the "midst [center] of all things" (D&C 88:13). The Kolob Theorem proposes this is in the center of the Milky Way Galaxy.

CHAPTER 4
INTERSTELLAR DUST SHIELDS EARTH FROM SEEING THE CENTER OF THE GALAXY OR HEAVEN

Natural man would "wither and die" in the presence of God, but if he looked with "spiritual eyes," as Moses did when God's glory came upon him, he could "behold his face, for I [Moses] was transfigured before him" (Moses 1:11). The glory, bright light and enormous radiations do proceed forth from God 'to fill the immensity of space' (D&C 88:12). Earth is hidden and protected from this burning glory by a veil of interstellar dust.

CHAPTER 5
WE CANNOT NUMBER ALL THE STARS AND PLANETS IN THE MILKY WAY, ALTHOUGH EACH ONE IS KNOWN TO GOD

God revealed to Moses that He had created "worlds without number" (Moses 1:33). Also "as one earth shall pass away . . . even so shall another come" (Moses 1:38). But the creation of worlds by God are but a secondary work. His primary focus and effort is the progress of His children. For God said "this is my work and my glory—to bring to pass the immortality and eternal life of man" (Moses 1:39). To accomplish this He has to build many suns and earths as residences for His many children. While men cannot count them, God knows each one and has given each one a name.

CHAPTER 6
A GALAXY CAN BE DIVIDED INTO THREE REGIONS

There are three degrees of glory in the resurrection described in wonderful detail (D&C 76). Paul identified these glories as being similar to the sun, moon and stars. (1 Cor. 15:40–42). Each of these three places, Celestial, Terrestrial and Telestial, will be the final residence of a part of mankind after the judgment and the resurrection. Their placement will be based on their works and faith while on earth. The location of each of these kingdoms of glory is in concentric rings in the Milky Way Galaxy with God's throne, the celestial kingdom, in the center.

CHAPTER 7
THERE IS A PLACE FOR "OUTER DARKNESS"

Location of outer darkness, the final place for the devil, his angels and the sons of perdition is theorized to be outside the limits of the Milky Way where it is dark and cold.

CHAPTER 8
THE EARTH IS ALIVE AND HAS FOLLOWED A SEQUENCE SIMILAR TO A HUMAN SOUL

The earth is alive and changes from time to time. The Lord explained "the earth abideth the law of a celestial kingdom, for it filleth the measure of its creation, and transgresseth not the law . . . notwithstanding it shall die, it shall be quickened again" (D&C 88:25–26).

The earth has a spirit for it was created spiritually before it became temporal (Moses 3:4–5). It was clothed with spiritual vegetation and animal life. Animals also have spirits (D&C 77:2, Moses 3:5). Next, the earth became a terrestrial Garden of Eden (Moses 3:8). After the fall of Adam, the earth became cursed or telestial, a fit place for mortal man (Moses 4:23–25) and subject to death. The Prophet Enoch, seventh from Adam, records he actually heard the earth speak, saying, "I [the earth] am pained . . . because of the wickedness of my children" (Moses 7:48). The earth also asked to be able to rest (Moses 7:48). This prayer of the earth will be answered after the second coming during the thousand year Millennium of peace (Moses 7:64). Finally the earth will be celestialized when it returns to its original orbit about Kolob.

CHAPTER 9
HEAVENLY FATHER HAS OTHER SPIRIT CHILDREN WHOM HE PLACES ON OTHER EARTHS IN THE MILKY WAY GALAXY

God's offspring are placed on other worlds as well as this earth (D&C 76:24, 88:51–57). Christ assisted the Father in the creation of all these worlds. Also Christ is the Savior and Redeemer of each of these other worlds. The Prophet Joseph taught us that the inhabitants of other worlds are "saved by the same Savior as ours." Also many of these worlds are now inhabited by Heavenly Father's other children.

CHAPTER 10
GOD AND SPIRIT BEINGS CAN MOVE AND COMMUNICATE AT VERY FAST SPEEDS

God manages His kingdom efficiently. He has a very fast means of communications and transportation; a speed much faster that light.

Travel between various places in God's kingdom can be done by spiritual beings at or near the speed of thought.

Time on earth (24 hours/day and 365 days/year) started with the fall of Adam (Abraham 5:13) and will end at the start of the Millennium (D&C 84:100). God's time passes much slower than mans'; in ratio as one is to 365,000 (Abraham Facsimile 2:1).

CHAPTER 11
THINGS ON EARTH ARE PATTERNED AFTER THINGS IN HEAVEN

Things on the temporal earth look like their counterparts which are spiritual, which God has created in heaven (D&C 77:2). Mankind, male and female, is created on the earth in the image and likeness of God in heaven (Geneses 1:27). Thus we can better understand spiritual and heavenly things by observing things on the earth, for the earth, and all in it, is in heaven's image and appearance.

CHAPTER 12
GOD HAS THE ABILITY TO FULFILL HIS PROMISES TO HIS FAITHFUL CHILDREN

God has promised "all he has" as an inheritance for his faithful children (D&C 84:38, 132:16–17, 29, 37). To receive all the Father has is to become a "god" (D&C 76:58). The plan of God's universe must include matter and space for these new inheritances to be organized and given to all who become exalted in the highest heaven. This does not mean that these faithful children will take the place of our Father in Heaven, but they become a god to their own spirit children (D&C 76:58; 132:20).

This idea is in sharp contrast of the current idea that Heaven is a blissful place, resting on billowy clouds, playing harps, singing praises. We reject this idea as being without family, without purpose, growth or achievement and quite stagnant.

CHAPTER 13
THE MANY GALAXIES WE SEE OUTSIDE THE MILKY WAY ARE NOT CREATED BY OUR HEAVENLY FATHER BUT BY OTHER GODS

Our father Eloheim, had a father. This revelation to the Prophet Joseph (although known before, Revelation 1:6), opens a window to understand the entire cosmos. Now we can visualize the whole picture; it stretches out before us in the form of billions of galaxies. There is no end to them regardless of what direction we look. When we see these galaxies, external to the Milky Way, we realize that they are not the creations of Eloheim but of his forefathers and relatives who are gods also. But to us there is only one God the Father and only one Lord Jesus Christ whom we worship.

Bibliography

Scriptural references are included in the body of the text. Quotations are selected from all the standard works of The Church of Jesus Christ of Latter-day Saints. The standard works include: Holy Bible, Book of Mormon, Doctrine and Covenants, and the Pearl of Great Price.

All other sources and authorities are listed below in this bibliography in alphabetical order. Where the entry is for an author, it is by the author's first name.

Bernhard, Bennett, Rice, *New Handbook of the Heavens* Hubert J. Bernhard, Dorothy A. Bennett and Hugh S. Rice: *Moon Stars Astronomy,* Whittlesey House, McGraw-Hill Company, New York, 1964.

B.H. Roberts, *The Gods and Their Government*, Contributor.

Bok and Bok, *The Milky Way* 5th Edition, Harvard University Press, Cambridge, MA, 1981.

Brigham Young, *Journal of Discourses.*

Brigham Young, *Deseret News* 16 Nov. 1859.

BYU Selected Speeches, 1951, J. Reuben Clark, Jr. "What Was This Jesus", published by BYU Extension Publications.

Chet Raymo, Starry Nights: *An Introduction to Astronomy for Every Night of the Year,* Prentice-Hall, Englewood Cliffs, New Jersey.

Colin A. Ronan, *Deep Space*, MacMillan Publishing Co., NY, 1982.

Deseret News.

Eliza R. Snow, *LDS Hymns,* 1891.

Franklin D. Richards and James A. Little, *Compendium of the Doctrines of the Gospel*, Salt Lake City, Deseret Book Company, 1925.

Fred Hoyle, *Frontiers of Astronomy*, New York, Harpers, 1955.

G. Neugebauer & Eric E. Becklin, "The Brightest Infrared Sources," *Scientific American*, April 1973.

George Reynolds and Janne M. Sjodahl, *Commentary on the Pearl of Great Price*, 1965.

Hal Knight, "Are There Millions of Earth-like Planets?," *Deseret News*, Feb. 2, 1966.

Harlow Shapley, *The Galaxies*, Harvard University Press, Cambridge, MA, 1961.

Heber C. Kimball, *Masterpieces of LDS Leaders*, N.B. Lundwall.

Hollis R. Johnson, "Civilizations Out in Space," *BYU Studies*, Autumn 1970.

Hymns of the Church of Jesus Christ of Latter-day Saints.

Isaac Asimov, *The Universe: From Flat Earth to Quasar*, Walker Company, NY, 1966.

James E. Talmage, *Improvement Era*, 1904.

John A. Widtsoe, *Discourses of Brigham Young*, Deseret Book Company, 1977.

John Taylor, *The Mormon*, August 29, 1857.

Joseph Ashbrook, "The Nucleus of the Andromeda Nebula," *Sky and Telescope*, February 1968.

Joseph Fielding Smith, *Doctrines of Salvation*, Bookcraft, 1955.

Joseph Fielding Smith, *Man: His Origin and Destiny*, 1954.

Joseph Smith, *Egyptian Alphabet and Grammar*, Utah Lighthouse Book Store, 135 SW Temple, Salt Lake City, Utah, 1966.

Joseph Smith, Quoted in the Contributor, October 1882 – September 1883.

Joseph Smith, *Times and Seasons*, August 1843.

M. Garfield Cook, *Everlasting Burnings*, Phoenix Publishing Inc., Salt Lake City, Utah, 1981.

Melvin J. Ballard, "The Path to Celestial Happiness," *Deseret News*.

Orson Pratt, *Formation of the Earth*, Elder's Journal.

Orson Pratt, *Journal of Discourses*

Orson Pratt, *March 14, 1875, Salt Lake City, 16th Ward*, reported by David W. Evans.

Orson Pratt, *Millennial Star*.

Parley P. Pratt, *Millennial Star*, Feb 1841.

Roy A. Gallant, *Exploring the Universe*, Garden City, New York: Garden City Books, 1956.

Teachings of the Prophet Joseph Smith.

Times and Seasons.

Walter Sullivan, "Balloon Data," *The New York Times*, April 27, 1978.

William W. Phelps, *Times and Seasons*, January 1, 1845.

About the Author

Lynn M. Hilton is known as a pathfinder and original thinker.

He was trained as a bomber pilot in the US Army Air Corps during World War II. After the war he served as a missionary in the New England States (1945–1947). He married and was sealed to Annalee Hope Avarell in 1948. He earned a PhD in the Department of Education from the University of Chicago in 1952.

He was a professor at Brigham Young University from 1953–1964. During his time at BYU he served as Associate Dean of Adult Education.

He served a term in the Utah House of Representatives.

He is the original discoverer of the Lehi Trail in Arabia (see *Ensign* Magazine "In Search of Lehi's Trail," September and October, 1976).

He worked four years in Egypt and seven years in Saudi Arabia.

His faithful wife Hope died in 1999 after a long illness. During his entire life he has served in many wards, stake and mission assignments for The Church of Jesus Christ of Latter-day Saints. He has four children and fourteen grandchildren.

Lynn married and was sealed to Nancy Mae Goldberg in the Salt Lake Temple in 2001 and since has completed three Senior Missions with her. They labored in Sydney Australia, The Church of Jesus Christ of Latter-day Saints Office Building, and Greece Athens Mission with assignments in Irbid, Jordan and Athens, Greece.

He is the author of many books and articles, several have been widely published.

Index